NOLS Cookery

NOLS Cookery

Claudia Pearson
Editor

Illustrations by Mike Clelland

STACKPOLE
BOOKS

Copyright © 1997 by Stackpole Books

Published by
STACKPOLE BOOKS
5067 Ritter Road
Mechanicsburg, PA 17055

Printed in The United States of America

10 9 8 7 6 5

Fourth edition

Library of Congress Cataloging-in-Publication Data

NOLS Cookery / [edited by] Claudia Pearson. — 4th ed.
     p.   cm.
   Includes index.
   ISBN 0-8117-2860-9
   1. Outdoor cookery. I. Lindholm, Claudia. 1955- II. National
Outdoor Leadership School (U.S.)
   TX823.N65   1997
   641.5'78—dc21   97-6633
                                                        CIP

Contents

Preface

Several factors were considered when we decided to revise *NOLS Cookery*. First, we needed to update some of the ingredients and recipes to reflect the food that is currently used by the National Outdoor Leadership School (NOLS). Second, specific recipe ingredients had to be edited to include a broader range of choices and to encourage creativity. And finally, due to a number of requests for bulk ration planning information, we decided to include a section explaining that system. For this edition, our ultimate goal was to create a cookbook that accomplished these three objectives. We wanted to create a complete field guide and workbook that was easy to use and encouraged creativity for both NOLS students and any backpacker who strives to cook nutritious and tasty meals in the wilderness.

All NOLS field rations based out of the Rocky Mountain branch in Lander, Wyoming, utilize the bulk ration planning system. This system of rationing uses a wide selection of bulk foods and spices figured on a pounds per person per day basis and distributed into individual groups of two to four people. Each group decides what to cook with the help of the *NOLS Cookery*, other knowledgeable peers, or instructors. On NOLS courses, students learn how to cook in the field through experience. On NOLS semester courses, students take this one step further and, following certain budgetary constraints and weight considerations, plan their own rations.

In this version of *NOLS Cookery*, we have provided the tools you need to plan a ration of your own. Successful ration planning takes both effort and experience, and, as many of you already know, it can be challenging and time-consuming. Critical factors to consider when planning for an expedition are the availability, versatility, cost, and palatability of foods desired. Happy campers must be well fed and hydrated. Plan on as much variety as possible, ask your trip members for their input, and prepare most of the food ahead of time to ensure ease of preparation once in the field. Our goal has always been to please each student and instructor just once on any expedition. That leaves quite a safety margin!

At NOLS, we strongly encourage experimenting, so feel free to make substitutions for specific ingredients. Don't overlook a recipe if you don't have the exact grain, nut, or flour that it calls for. Many of the revisions have eliminated the rigid structures of the recipes. For example, we no longer rely on specific types of fruit, such as apples, for cobbler. Instead, the cobbler recipe calls for dried fruit. Less structured recipes foster creativity. Many of our best meals have been discovered through trial and error. Our motto is that your imagination is your only limitation, so experiment and share what you have created!

—*Claudia Pearson,*
Marlo Garnsworthy,
and Cindy Rhines

Acknowledgments

As with previous editions of *NOLS Cookery*, countless students, instructors, and in-town staff contributed ideas and recipes to this edition. Many people brought in recipes claiming that when they were cooked in the field, they were some of the best meals they had ever eaten. We chuckled (knowing what hunger, high altitude, and fatigue can do to one's judgment), grabbed their recipes, and assembled them in the Gourmet Gulch test kitchen. We shared these creations with branch staff and fall semester graduates who, after ninety-plus days on NOLS rations, were still enthusiastic taste testers. We laughed, cooked, and ate our way through December and, in the end, came up with some great additions to this book. Each new recipe has so many variations that it would be difficult not to please even the pickiest eaters.

I would like to thank the original editors and contributors to previous *Cookery* editions. Their knowledge and ideas remain a fundamental part of this book.

For this edition, I would like to credit the following people who put their time and energy into making a great cookbook:

To Molly Absolon, who brought us together and formally got us going on this project. Molly, a NOLS instructor and author, helped us immensely with the organization and the mission of this book.

To Tod Schimelpfenig, who took parts of the text and, with his special knack, tightened up the wording (a skill learned from tightening too many budgets).

To Marlo Garnsworthy, our fiery Australian intern who charged from computer to computer during the busy fall semester to edit many chapters with relentless enthusiasm. Marlo, who had been a semester student in the spring of 1996 and had used the book extensively during her course, provided some realistic and candid evaluations of recipes and methods based on her experience.

To Cindy Rhines, my assistant, who single-handedly ran the Gulch while I spent hours at the computer writing and rewriting various chapters. Cindy was an invaluable proofreader who checked my wording, spelling, and punctuation daily. Cindy was also the head chef when we started to test recipes.

To Donna Orr, a gifted writer, friend, and previous author of *NOLS Cookery*, who offered suggestions that helped me gain a sense of clarity in my writing. She was also helpful with the shopping list.

To Sam Talucci, instructor and restaurateur, who took a copy of the book home with him after instructing all summer and made suggestions for this new version.

To Mike Clelland, a NOLS instructor and the illustrator of this book, whose humor inspired me and made me realize how useful it can be as a teaching tool.

To Shana Tarter, Peggy Savanick, Mark Herrlinger, Lisa Jaeger, Jon Kempsey, Molly Doran, and the many instructors and student groups who submitted recipes for testing. And finally, to anyone else who wandered into the NOLS test kitchen and said, "Well, I do it this way . . . ," thanks.

Claudia Pearson

planning

RATION PLANNING

Each year, approximately 2,600 students attend NOLS courses. The majority of these courses last thirty-one days. How does NOLS plan meals for so many people over such a long period? Each course is divided into cook groups of two to four individuals, and each cook group is given a wide selection of bulk foods and spices. There are no set menus. The students decide what meals to prepare with the raw materials they are provided.

We call this method NOLS bulk rationing and have found that this system works well for our multiweek expeditions. Smaller groups going out for shorter lengths of time—five days or less—might want to consider menu planning instead. With menu planning, all meals are determined in advance, and the food is bought accordingly.

If you have always used menu planning, bulk rationing may be a difficult concept to grasp at first, but the rewards can be great once you've mastered the basics. Planning and packing become easier. Complicated lists and menu schedules are eliminated. You'll have greater freedom in the field to prepare meals that suit your mood and the demands of the day. Cooking becomes more creative and flexible when you carry a "backcountry pantry" in your pack.

Factors to consider when ration planning:
- Group size
- Duration of trip
- Purpose of trip
- Exertion level
- Weather

- Altitude
- Individual appetites
- Food preferences within the group
- Nutritional balance
- Expense and availability
- Spoilage and ease of packaging
- Weight
- Possible dietary limitations of group members

NOLS Rationing System

The first step in planning food for an expedition using the NOLS bulk rationing method is to calculate the total amount of food that will be needed during the trip. To do this, determine how many pounds (of food) per person per day (ppppd) you expect to use. This amount depends on everything from the intensity and duration of the trip to the ages and sizes of the participants. Charts and worksheets are included in this chapter to help you determine this figure.

Once you have figured out the total poundage, break it down into different food groups to get specific amounts. NOLS issues a combination of heavier "grocery store" foods and lighter dehydrated items.

Freeze-dried meals available at backpacking and sporting goods stores are lightweight and quick to cook, but they are often bland and expensive. If you decide to purchase freeze-dried foods, be forewarned that the suggested serving sizes should be doubled for most appetites. And beware, they tend to be high in salt. Freeze-dried food used in conjunction with staples can provide variety and save weight.

You can find many tasty, lightweight, nutritious, and inexpensive options at your local supermarket, natural foods store, or specialty market. Food dryers are a wonderful addition to any kitchen. They are available in most hardware, discount, or kitchen supply stores. A large variety of home-grown or store-bought fresh vegetables, fruits, and meats can be dried, providing tasty, affordable, and nutritious additions to a backpacker's menu. There are many books available on drying and dehydrating foods at the local library. You can even dry foods in your own oven.

Make note of the food preferences and allergies within your group, and avoid letting your personal likes and dislikes influence your choices. Variety is important and will help keep morale up. Balance expensive and less expensive items by using a predetermined budget.

Bulk Ration Planning Steps

Step 1: *Determine the amount of food per person per day (ppppd), using the following guidelines:*

- 1.5 ppppd is appropriate for hot days and warm nights. This amount works well when base camping (camping in one location for the duration of the trip) and is good for short trips (three to five days) when fresh veggies, canned goods, and/or fresh fish supplement the ration. An excellent amount for trips with children and for leisure days, 1.5 pounds equates to roughly 2,500 to 3,000 calories per person per day.
- 1.75 to 2 pppd works well when you expect warm or cool days and nights or when hiking with full packs. If you are planning a long trip of more than seven to ten days, you might want to plan on 2 ppppd for later in the ration period, since appetites usually kick in after a few days in the mountains. For moderate to active work-days, 1.75 to 2 pounds is ideal and gives you roughly 3,000 to 3,500 calories per person.

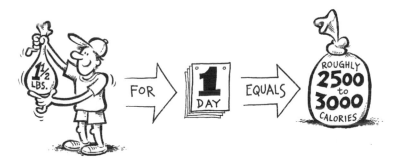

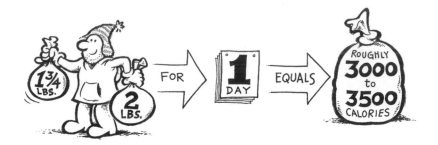

- 2 to 2.25 ppppd is good for hiking or skiing with full packs during the cool days and cold nights of early spring, late fall, or winter. If you are planning a long trip of more than seven to ten days, you might want to plan on 2.25 ppppd for later in the ration period. Two to 2.25 pounds per day is ideal for heavy workdays and cold temperatures. It gives you roughly 3,500 to 4,500 calories per person per day.
- 2.5 ppppd is good for cold days and extremely cold nights, such as in midwinter, when you are skiing with full packs or sleds in mountain environments. Used for extremely strenuous workdays and very cold temperatures, 2.5 pounds gives you roughly 4,000 to 5,000 calories per person per day.

Step 2: *Figure the total amount of food needed for the trip.* The formula is: Number of people × number of days × ppppd. For example, for four people on an eight-day trip at 1.75 ppppd, the total amount of food needed would equal 56 pounds.

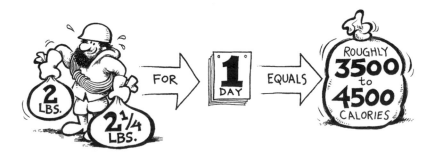

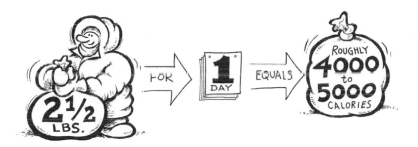

Step 3: *Break the total poundage into food groups.* The following chart lists the breakdown of the poundage of different foods per person per day. Added together, these numbers should equal the pounds per person per day selected in step 1. These food category breakdowns have proved effective in planning NOLS rations for many years.

	Breakdown of Pounds per Person per Day from				
	1.5 ppppd	1.75 ppppd	2 ppppd	2.25 ppppd	2.5 ppppd
Food Category					
Breakfast	.24	.28	.33	.35	.38
Dinner	.27	.32	.35	.37	.40
Cheese	.19	.22	.24	.26	.28
Trail foods	.32	.35	.37	.45	.49
Flour and baking*	.11	.13	.16	.09	.10
Sugar and fruit drinks	.10	.12	.14	.15	.18
Soups, bases, desserts	.06	.09	.13	.15	.19
Milk, eggs, margarine, cocoa	.21	.24	.28	.31	.33
Meats and substitutes†	0	0	0	.12	.15

*The need for baking ingredients is lower in winter conditions, when only quick pan baking is feasible.
†High-fat and high-preservative meats are added in winter to meet higher fuel needs.

Step 4: *Calculate the total pounds of each food category needed for the trip.* Using the example from step 2 of four people on an eight-day trip at 1.75 ppppd and the values from the table in step 3, the calculations would be as follows:

Food Category	Calculation	Rounded
Trail foods	.35 × 4 × 8 = 11.2 lbs.	11 lbs.
Dinner	.32 × 4 × 8 = 10.24 lbs.	10.5 lbs.
Breakfast	.28 × 4 × 8 = 8.96 lbs.	9 lbs.
Milk, eggs, margarine, cocoa	.24 × 4 × 8 = 7.68 lbs.	7.5 lbs
Cheese	.22 × 4 × 8 = 7.04 lbs.	7 lbs.
Flour and baking	.13 × 4 × 8 = 4.16 lbs.	4 lbs.
Sugar and fruit drinks	.12 × 4 × 8 = 3.84 lbs.	4 lbs.
Soups, bases, desserts	.09 × 4 × 8 = 2.88 lbs.	3 lbs.
Meats and substitutes	NOLS only uses in 2.25–2.5 lb rations	
Total pounds		56 lbs.

Step 5: *Round the numbers up or down within categories (see the last column of the table in step 4) and make substitutions, depending on individual preferences.* For instance, if you don't want to bake, you can take that poundage (approximately 4 pounds in the example) and add it to another category such as breakfast or dinner. If you don't eat cheese, you can take some of that cheese weight (approximately 7 pounds in this example) and add it to the trail food category, where you can replace it with nuts and/or nut butters (sesame, peanut, tahini, almond). The important thing to remember is to make exchanges with similar types of foods to maintain the balance among carbohydrates, proteins, and fats. If you make changes, the adjusted totals should still equal the amount determined in step 2.

The following worksheet can be used to plan your own ration.

Ration Planning Worksheet

If you have already chosen your pounds per person per day (ppppd), you are ready to fill in the worksheet.

Take the number of days × number of people × ppppd = total weight for chosen ration period

$$\underline{\hspace{2cm}} \times \underline{\hspace{2cm}} \times \underline{\hspace{2cm}} = \underline{\hspace{2cm}}$$
$$\text{(days)} \qquad \text{(people)} \qquad \text{(ppppd)} \qquad \text{(total weight)}$$

Break down total weight into food categories (see step 3 in text)

Category	No. of People	×	No. of Days	×	ppppd	=	Total lbs. for Category
Breakfast	_____	×	_____	×	_____	=	_____
Dinner	_____	×	_____	×		=	
Cheese	_____	×	_____	×	_____	=	_____
Trail foods	_____	×	_____	×	_____	=	_____
Flour and baking	_____	×	_____	×	_____	=	_____
Sugar and fruit drinks	_____	×	_____	×	_____	=	_____
Soups, bases, desserts	_____	×	_____	×	_____	=	_____
Milk, eggs, margarine, cocoa	_____	×	_____	×	_____	=	_____
Meats and substitutes	_____	×	_____	×	_____	=	_____
					Total weight =		_____

List specific foods that you would like to take under each category listed below. You have generated these category totals in the formulas above.

Breakfast Item/lbs.	Dinner Item/lbs.	Cheese Item/lbs.	Trail Foods Item/lbs.	Flour and Baking Item/lbs.
_____	_____	_____	_____	_____
_____	_____	_____	_____	_____
_____	_____	_____	_____	_____
_____	_____	_____	_____	_____
_____	_____	_____	_____	_____
_____	_____	_____	_____	_____
_____	_____	_____	_____	_____
_____	_____	_____	_____	_____
Total lbs. ____	Total lbs. ____	Total lbs. ____	Total lbs. ____	Total lbs. ____

Sugar and Fruit Drinks Item/lbs.	Soups, Bases, Desserts Item/lbs.	Milk, Eggs, Margarine, Cocoa Item/lbs.	Meats and Substitutes Item/lbs.
_____	_____	_____	_____
_____	_____	_____	_____
_____	_____	_____	_____
_____	_____	_____	_____
_____	_____	_____	_____
_____	_____	_____	_____
_____	_____	_____	_____
_____	_____	_____	_____
Total lbs. ____	Total lbs. ____	Total lbs. ____	Total lbs. ____

Here at NOLS, we issue spice kits, tea bags, base packs, canned goods, fresh vegetables, toilet paper, matches, and soap (liquid or bar), in addition to the total weight planned for each ration. Make sure you include your choice of these items for your personal trips.

NUTRITION AND QUANTITIES

Staying healthy, strong, warm, cheerful, and alert helps ensure the success of your expedition. All these things depend on eating properly. Therefore, having a basic understanding of nutrition is essential to putting together a healthy backcountry ration.

Nutritionists today recognize four basic food groups and one additional category:

1. The **milk group** supplies calcium, riboflavin (vitamin B_2), and protein. Cheese, milk, cocoa, cheesecake, and puddings fall in this category. (Two to three servings per day)
2. The **meat group** supplies protein, niacin, iron, and thiamine (vitamin B_1) for muscle, bone, blood cells, and healthy skin and nerves. Peanut butter, eggs, beans, legumes, and nuts fall in this category. (Two to three servings per day)
3. The **fruit and vegetable group** supplies vitamin A and vitamin C for night vision, resistance to infections, and help in healing wounds. Potatoes, freeze-dried vegetables, tomato base, fortified fruit drinks, dried fruit, and wild edibles fall in this category. (Five to nine servings per day)
4. The **grain group** supplies carbohydrates, thiamine, iron, and niacin for energy and a healthy nervous system. Flour, pasta, rice, cereals, couscous, and bulgur fall in this category. (Four servings per day)
5. **Other foods** complement but don't replace foods from

the four basic groups. These include sweets, fats and oils, coffee, tea, and condiments. Since these foods provide calories in addition to those contained in the basic four, amounts are determined by individual needs.

You should eat a wide variety of food from the five groups each day to get the nutrients you need. Nutrients can be grouped into six classes:

1. **Protein** is necessary to build body cells. Since your cells are constantly being replaced, you need to eat protein your entire life. Proteins are made up of amino acids. Animal proteins (meat, cheese, milk) supply amino acids in the right proportions for your body to use. Proteins from plant foods (beans, legumes, grains) usually lack some indispensable amino acid. These foods are called incomplete proteins. By combining certain incomplete proteins, you can produce a complete protein. Some successful combinations are beans and rice, peanuts and wheat, and macaroni and cheese. Ten to 15 percent of your daily intake of food should be made up of proteins.

2. **Carbohydrates** are the starches and sugars in plant foods. During exercise, you burn carbohydrates. The more you exercise, the more carbohydrate-rich foods you need. A high-carbohydrate diet means eating a variety of vegetables, whole grains, legumes, and fruits. These foods supply complex carbohydrates and also provide fiber. Sugar consumption is *not* necessarily synonymous with instant energy, nor is it a source of complex carbohydrates. Fifty-five to 80 percent of your daily intake of food should be made up of carbohydrates.

3. **Fats** take longer for your body to digest in comparison to other nutrients. They provide energy after the quicker-burning carbohydrates have been used up.

Approximately 30 percent of your daily intake of food should be made up of fats, of which only 10 percent should be saturated fat.

4. **Vitamins** have no caloric value but are essential for your body to function properly. The average person eating a balanced and varied diet does not need vitamin supplements.

5. **Minerals** help in many physiological functions. They come from the foods you eat and the water you drink.

6. **Water** makes up approximately 60 percent of your body weight. Your body's need for water increases with exercise due to losses through sweating and breathing. In the summer, drink a minimum of 2 to 3 quarts per day; in winter, 3 to 4 quarts; and at altitude—more than 7,000 feet—3 to 5 quarts. Dehydration causes headaches, muscle cramps, and nausea and can increase your susceptibility to hypothermia, frostbite, and altitude sickness.

The energy for everything you do is obtained from the food you eat. Calories are simply a measurement of that energy. Proteins and carbohydrates each supply roughly 112 calories per ounce. Fat is a more concentrated source of energy and supplies approximately 252 calories per ounce.

SAMPLE SHOPPING LIST

Note: Some items are available through mail-order from the NOLS Rocky Mountain Branch Rations Department, 502 Lincoln Street Lander, Wyoming 82520; 307-332-1419.

Breakfast

Cereals are a good source of carbohydrates and are high in protein when mixed with milk. Adding margarine or nuts to cereals provides fats and additional protein.

- **Cream of Wheat, Rice, or Rye; oatmeal; hominy grits.** Hot cereals are available in many forms: regular or instant, in bulk or individual packets. Some cereals come presweetened; others can be mixed with sugar, dried fruits, nuts, milk, and margarine for breakfast. Cereals such as oatmeal can be used in baked goods or in casseroles for dinner meals. Grits should be cooked and allowed to sit for a while before serving. They can then be refried and served with hot sauce or picante, lots of cheese, and pepper.
- **Couscous.** Couscous is available in two types: the whole wheat version, which is less processed and is a light brown color, or the more refined and traditional version, which is yellow. Both types cook fast and can be hydrated and eaten right out of your camp cup. Couscous can be mixed with sweetener, dried fruits, and nuts for a hot breakfast or combined with cheese and veggies for a tasty dinner.
- **Hash-brown potatoes—dried or shredded.** Hash browns make an excellent breakfast or dinner. They are

best served in fried form with cheese and seasonings, or with bacon or sausage for a hearty winter meal.

- **Granola or muesli.** Many varieties of granola and muesli are available commercially, or you can make your own. Granola and muesli make a good breakfast served hot or cold. They can also be used as a trail food or an ingredient in dessert crusts or can be added to baked goods or cookies.
- **Cold cereals.** Cold cereals can be used for breakfast, as a snack food, or as ingredients in desserts or baked goods. (The bulky nature of some cereals can be a problem for packing, however.)
- **Pancake mix/baking mix.** Make your own baking mix or use a quick add-water-only commercial brand.
- **Bagels, English muffins, muffins, coffee cake, quick breads.** Bread products are available commercially, or you can make your own. They are great for breakfast, trail foods, and dinner.

Dinner

Pasta, grains, and potatoes are good sources of carbohydrates. The addition of beans or dairy products to these items makes complete proteins, and cheese and margarine provide added protein and fats.

- **Pasta.** Pastas are made from white and whole grain flours and come in a wide variety of shapes and colors. Pasta is a popular dinner food, that can be used in many recipes from soups to casseroles.
- **Instant beans.** Pinto and black beans are available dried or refried in most big grocery stores or natural food shops. Beans are great with tortillas or rice or in combination with pasta. Leftovers make good dips or spreads with crackers or tortillas.
- **Instant lentils.** Lentils are good with rice, in soups, or to make vegetarian burgers. They are available in most natural food stores.

- **Falafel.** Instant falafel can be mixed with water, formed into patties, and fried as a veggie burger served with rice or bread. It is very spicy!
- **Barley.** Quick-cooking barley is a good ingredient in soups or mixed with various grains for a main meal.
- **Hummus.** Hummus makes an excellent dip or spread with crackers or pita bread.
- **Couscous.** Excellent as a main dish for breakfast or dinner. Couscous is very versatile.
- **Bulgur.** Bulgur is nice in soups or mixed with other grains. Bulgur is the main ingredient in tabouli, a popular cold Lebanese salad. It can be used in many ways, from baked goods to breakfast.
- **Instant potato pearls or flakes.** Instant potatoes make a good thickener for soups and gravies. They are also excellent served alone or as an addition to a main meal. Cooked with cheese, margarine, and a cup-of-soup packet, instant potatoes make a quick mini-meal. They can also be used for a savory breakfast or mixed with flour to make potato pancakes.
- **Rice—white, brown, parboiled.** Rice is a versatile mainstay and is available in many varieties. Instant rice cooks the fastest and mixes well with lentils or beans.
- **Textured vegetable protein.** Textured vegetable protein is made from soybeans mixed with other ingredients to make a veggie burger or chili mix. It is a good source of protein for vegetarians.
- **Tortillas, pita breads, bagels, biscuits, flat breads.** These products are great additions to main meals or as ready-to-eat snacks for the trail. However, they can be bulky and are perishable.

Cheese

Cheese is a good source of protein and fats. Farmer, jack, cheddar, Swiss, mozzarella, and Parmesan are popular varieties. In winter, cube all cheeses for easy melting. Purchase cheese in vacuum-sealed blocks and open one at a time to ensure freshness.

Trail Foods

Trail food consists of high-calorie, tasty foods that are easy to eat while hiking on the trail. Nuts and seeds contain protein and fats, and dried fruits, crackers, and energy bars provide carbohydrates and fiber.

- **Nuts.** Nuts are available in most big grocery stores or natural food outlets. They are an expensive but concentrated form of calories. Roasted and salted nuts and seeds taste great but can go rancid quickly without refrigeration. Raw forms can be bland and chewy but perk up nicely when dry roasted and salted prior to eating. Nuts are a nice ingredient for main dishes or in baked goods. Choose from the many varieties available, use nut mixes, or try products such as gorp—a mix of nuts, fruits, and candy.
- **Seeds—roasted or raw.** Pumpkin, sunflower, sesame, and piñon seeds are popular and can be eaten plain or added to breakfasts, dinners, and baked goods.
- **Dried fruits.** Dried fruits are an expensive but concentrated form of calories easily found in grocery and natural food stores. For trips that require large quantities of trail food, try purchasing fresh fruit at a fraction of the cost and drying it on your own using a food dryer. This system also works well for vegetables such as tomatoes, zucchini, and mushrooms. Dried fruit options include individual fruits and berries, mixed fruit combinations, and fruit leathers.
- **Crackers.** Crackers come in countless varieties and are available everywhere. Pack them in plastic containers with peel-off lids for protection. Occasional crunchy foods are usually welcome on long trips. Crackers are great for dips and spreadables such as cheese and nut butters and hummus. Choose from flavored and shaped

crackers, melba toasts, bagel chips, pretzels, and croutons.

- **Corn nuts and soy nuts.** Corn nuts and soy nuts are salty, crunchy, and cheap, with a strong flavor. But you need to be careful with them—they can break teeth. Soybeans are an excellent form of protein.
- **Cookies.** Cookies come in various types and flavors. Fruit Newtons, fruit boosters, animal crackers, granola bars, and Pop Tarts hold up well in a backpack.
- **Energy bars.** Numerous varieties of energy bars such as Power, Stoker, Clif, Pemmican, and Tiger's Milk are available for quick pick-me-ups or meal replacement. Make sure that they are edible in cold weather conditions—don't break a tooth.
- **Candy.** Backpacking favorites include candy bars, chocolate- or yogurt-covered nuts and fruits, and wrapped hard candies (remove wrappers as you bag them to prevent litter).

Baking Items

- **Powdered eggs.** Whole powdered eggs are useful for baking or in quiches and omelets. They are less appealing for use as scrambled eggs. Powdered eggs lighten up many recipes.
- **Flours/meal.** Choose from white, whole wheat, and other flours; cornmeal and tortilla mixes such as masa harina (flour) or mast trego (corn); and various commercial baking, biscuit, muffin, and pancake mixes.

Sugar and Powdered Fruit Drinks

- Brown and white sugar (brown is less likely to be confused with other foods).
- Lemonade (pink or yellow).
- Mixes such as Tang, apple cider, Gatorade, Kool-Aid.
- Jell-O gelatin (makes great hot drink).
- Teas—bags or instant powder varieties.

Soups, Bases, Dried Vegetables, and Desserts

- **Soups**
  - —Cup-of-soups: Many varieties of cup-of-soup are available. They can be added to potato pearls and cheese cubes to make a quick hot meal.
  - —Ramen soups: Ramen soups are tasty and nutritious when mixed with canned meats or cheeses to make a complete meal. They have a high fat content because the noodles are fried before being dried. Ramen is quick and easy to make.
  - —Bulk or individual soup bases such as chicken, beef, veggie, and miso are good for seasoning. Adding bases can help extend the life of your spice kit.
- **Bases**
  - —Tomato base: Complete tomato product in powdered form.
  - —Packaged sauce and seasoning mixes: Some choices are white, cheese, spaghetti, chili, pesto, and Alfredo sauces and gravies. Sauce packets are great to use with pasta.
- **Dried vegetables.** Dried veggies are an excellent way to add color and texture to colorless entrées. Mixed vegetables, green and red bell peppers, peas, and carrots are all used at NOLS. They are not included in the ration weights because they are issued in very small quantities and go a long way.
- **Desserts.** Desserts are high in carbohydrates, easy to digest, and, when milk products are added, good sources of protein. The easiest option is to buy premade dessert mixes that require only water.
  - —Cheesecake mix: Grapenuts, granola, or graham crackers make good crusts.
  - —Brownie mix: Great scrambled for quick gratification or used as an ingredient for fudge and specialty cakes.

—Gingerbread mix: Excellent added to flour for coffee
cakes and pancakes.

—Carrot cake mix: Many mixes come with cream
cheese frosting.

—Instant pudding or gelatin mixes.

Milk, Eggs, Margarine, and Cocoa

Milk and eggs are good sources of complete proteins. Cocoa
has milk and sugar as ingredients. Margarine is a good source
of fat.

- **Powdered milk.** Adding cold water works best.
- **Soy milk.** Soy milk is now available for vegetarians. At
  NOLS, we use Souvex Better than Milk brand. Many
  varieties are available, but taste test before your trip to
  make sure that you like it. You can combine chocolate
  and vanilla flavors to use as a cocoa replacement or use
  them separately. Carob flavor is also available.
- **Powdered eggs.** Whole powdered eggs.
- **Margarine.** Any kind of margarine works well. Beware
  of freeze or melt conditions and package accordingly.
  Squeeze tubes and containers with resealable peel-off
  lids work well but can open under pressure. Keep packaging easy, convenient, and tight.
- **Cocoa.** Instant bulk cocoa is a popular hot drink. You
  can stretch it by adding powdered milk.
- **Flavored coffee drinks.** These are popular with adults.
  They can be added to hot milk and cocoa for variety.
- **Coffee.** Many people like to carry grounds and use a
  coffee sock as a filter. Others use paper filters and cones
  or make Cowboy Coffee (see page 57). Instant coffee
  works well in winter conditions, when convenience is
  so important. Whatever your morning ritual, choose
  the form that works best for your group. Coffee is not a
  standard issue item at NOLS because of its diuretic
  effect.

Meats and Meat Substitutes

Meat, soybean products, and nut butters are all excellent sources of fat for the high energy demands of winter environments.

- **Sliced pepperoni, cooked bacon bits (real), and sausage crumbles.** These are all good for winter because they can withstand freeze-thaw conditions, are precooked, and are very flavorful.
- **Beef jerky.** Jerky is lightweight and tasty but does not have the high fat content that the meats listed above have.
- **Tempeh.** This is a soybean product that takes on the texture of meat and is used by many NOLS instructors as a meat or cheese replacement. It is perishable and must be watched for freshness. Tempeh is available in many flavors and can be used on short trips or as a meat replacement in the winter. It's best to cube the tempeh prior to using it on winter trips.
- **Nut butters.** These are commonly used to replace cheese and meat for vegetarians in the winter months. They are high in fat and protein and work well in winter conditions. Cashew, sesame, almond, and sunflower butters along with dried raisins and dates are a great alternative to meats and cheeses if you choose not to eat animal products and want to stay warm.

Spices

A spice kit is an important part of any cooking expedition. But remember that not everyone has the same tastes, so proceed with caution. Your spice kit might include the following:

- **Salt.** Used to add flavor to a flat-tasting meal.
- **Pepper.** Enhances most main dishes; tends to be a little hot.
- **Garlic powder.** Flavoring for breads, main dishes, soups, and sauces.
- **Chili powder.** Hot and spicy; good for Mexican dishes.

- **Curry.** Can be hot and spicy; used in Middle Eastern dishes.
- **Cinnamon.** Great for sweet breads and desserts.
- **Spike.** Lemon-salt flavor appeals to many palates; great in cheesy casseroles or spinkled on tortillas.
- **Oregano.** Good for Italian tomato sauces or casserole garnish.
- **Basil.** Used in tomato or white sauces.
- **Baking powder.** A quick leavening agent.
- **Baking yeast.** Great for breads, rolls, and pizza.
- **Cumin powder.** Used in rice or Mexican bean dishes.
- **Powdered mustard.** Good for white sauces or in grain and cheese casseroles.
- **Dill weed.** Excellent in soups, breads, muffins, or with fish.
- **Cayenne.** Very hot and spicy; used in sauces.

Liquids
- **Oil.** Good for sautéing or frying.
- **Vinegar.** Great for salad dressings, picante sauce, and other sauces.
- **Soy sauce.** Good over grains or in white sauces.
- **Vanilla.** Good for sweet baked goods, desserts, hot cereals, and drinks.
- **Tabasco/hot sauce.** A condiment for grains, pastas, and soups.

PACKAGING

The first thing to do once you have assembled all your food is to repackage it. Cardboard, paper, foil, and cans are all excess weight and potential litter.

At NOLS, we use two-ply clear plastic bags to package almost all our food. We purchase commercial bags that can be lightly tied in a knot. Plastic bags are lightweight and reusable and allow you to see what's inside. Use a permanent marker to identify contents if you're packing your own food.

We use small plastic bottles with screw-on lids for spices, and widemouthed Nalgene containers for honey, peanut butter, and margarine. Other possible food containers include Ziploc bags, freezer bags, Seal-a-Meal bags, Tupperware, and squeeze tubes.

If you are using a meal planning system, you may want to package each day's meals together or pack breakfasts, lunches, and dinners together by meal type. Label with a permanent marker and include recipe instructions.

Always be careful when packaging food to avoid any chance of contamination by soap, stove fuel, or a leaking

*Repackaged food
in zippered
carrying bag*

Don't pull the knots on plastic food bags too tight!

lighter. Try to keep the food above these items in your pack. Heavy items such as food should generally be high and close to your body, unless you'll be hiking through boulder fields or deadfall. In these conditions, carry most of the weight lower, for better balance when jumping or twisting.

Food should be packed above possible contaminants such as fuel or soap.

Heavy items packed high and
close to the body

Heavy items packed lower
to the body for better balance

RATION RESUPPLY

At NOLS, each student carries his or her share of the rations inside a 22-inch nylon zippered duffel bag. We find that a ten-day food supply (15 to 20 pounds) is the optimal amount people can carry comfortably. For longer trips, you have to plan a resupply.

There are a number of ways to resupply an expedition:

- *Roadhead resupply.* Make a loop back to the car, have a second car, or arrange for a friend to meet you with a ration at a roadhead.
- *Commercial packers or outfitters.* Commercial packers or outfitters (canoe liveries, river guides, horsepackers, and the like) can deliver rations to a predetermined point at a predetermined time. Price, weight limits, and packaging requirements vary.
- *Pack animals.* Backpacking with burros, horses, llamas, or goats is an option that allows you to carry more weight. Most public lands require special grazing permits for pack animals, so check the regulations. You should have experience packing and handling these animals before hitting the trail.
- *Mailing.* Mail yourself rations care of General Delivery to a post office in a town near your route. Be sure to include a "to be picked up by" date.
- *Caches.* Caches are illegal in many areas, so check the regulations. If caches are permissible, they should be put in waterproof, animal-proof containers.
- *Airdrops.* Airdrops are also illegal in many areas. Check with local authorities and your pilot first. Food for an

airdrop needs to be packaged so that the bags won't burst. Double box the food in cardboard boxes that are packed tightly and reinforced with strapping tape. Be sure the box will fit out the airplane window.

Regardless of how you choose to reration, a few guidelines must be followed. Have all information in writing concerning where and when you want the food delivered. Make a copy for both you and your resupplier. Mark locations on topographic maps. Make arrangements with the resupplier concerning what will happen if you don't get to the resupply point on time. Have this information in writing also. Be sure to check references if you are hiring a resupplier.

Food for rerationing should be bagged, boxed, weighed, and labeled for the resupplier. Do not depend on the resupplier to do your shopping and packaging. Be sure that the resupply point is completely cleaned up when you leave.

Hint: For any type of resupply, pack food so that loss of one box does not mean the complete loss of one type of food. Pack matches in plastic containers and in several places so they can't ignite by rubbing against each other.

cooking

EQUIPMENT AND STOVES

At NOLS, we have learned to produce gourmet meals with a minimum of cooking utensils. Each student has a bowl, a mug (usually an insulated 12- or 20-ounce cup with a lid), and a spoon. Each cook group is issued one or two (2- or 4-quart) nesting stainless-steel pots, one nonstick or 12-inch fry pan with a flat lid and no plastic parts, one spatula, one large spoon, one collapsible 6-quart or 1½- to 2½-gallon water jug or water bag, and pliers/pot grips. Optional luxuries include a small cheese grater, a small whisk for blending sauces, and a folding grate.

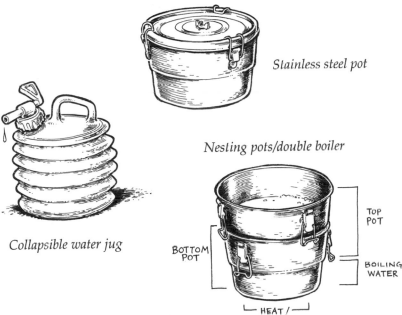

Stainless steel pot

Collapsible water jug

Nesting pots/double boiler

TOP POT

BOTTOM POT

BOILING WATER

⌐ HEAT ! ⌐

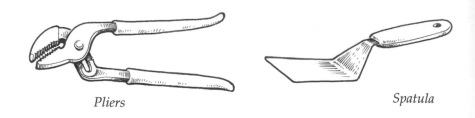

Pliers

Spatula

Large spoon

NOLS cup, spoon, and bowl

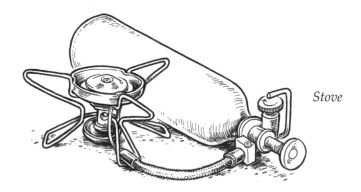

Stove

There are a number of excellent backpacking stoves on the market today. The most practical ones use white gas. However, white gas (Coleman fuel) is not always available in foreign countries. If this is a concern, interchangeable parts are available for some stoves that allow you to use kerosene. At NOLS, we use mainly Mountain Safety Research (MSR) Whisper Lite Internationale 600 stoves. These stoves are lightweight, easy to repair, relatively inexpensive, and reliable.

Have a clear understanding of how your stove works before you leave home. Carry the parts and tools necessary to repair it in an emergency. Keep it clean and dry, and clean the orifice after each use.

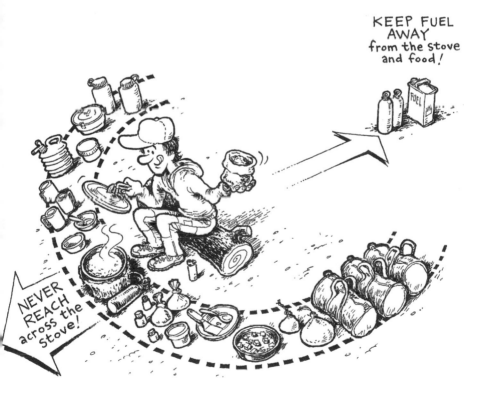

Keeping things organized in the cooking area will prevent accidents and surprises.

Locate your stove on a level surface protected from the wind and away from any vegetation. Watch out for sand and dirt that can clog the orifice or fuel line. If you are traveling in an area where it is impossible to get out of the sand or where you will be in snow, consider taking a stove pad or a piece of fire cloth to cook on. Position the stove with the on-off valve accessible. Keep the area clear of all burnable materials.

Store fuel in fuel bottles, and use funnels or pouring spouts to fill your stove. Fill stoves away from your cooking area and any open flames. Stoves should be filled after each use once they're cool. You never know when you'll have to start one in a hurry.

Figuring fuel amounts: During the summer with the Whisper Lites, we expect to use ½ liter of fuel per stove per day (based on a three-person cook group). *Example:* 1 stove × 8 days × ½ = 2.6 liters. During the winter, if you'll be melting

ONE
GALLON

3.7 liters
4 quarts
(128 oz.)

ONE
LITER

.946 quarts
(approx. ONE quart)

Fuel amounts vary depending on group size, time of year, and length of outing.

snow for water (or if you'll be at altitudes over 10,000 feet), plan on ¾ liter per stove per day, then round up the total to the next highest liter (based on a three-person cook group). If you round up your fuel amounts, you will have enough to run a small lantern—which is a definite plus during the long nights of winter.

COOKING ON FIRES

Campfires used to be a necessity in the backcountry; now they are usually a luxury. The growing number of backcountry travelers has resulted in the depletion of firewood in many areas, and the abuse of fire has caused everything from scarring to wildfires. Abuse is the key word here. Built properly, campfires can still be an enjoyable part of backcountry camping and cooking, but the decision to build one should never be made automatically or lightly. Regulations, ecological conditions, weather, skill, use level, and firewood availability should be considered when making the decision.

In a heavily used area, the best site for a fire is in an existing fire ring. In a pristine area, use Leave No Trace fire techniques. These techniques enable you to enjoy a fire without leaving any evidence. One quick, minimum-impact method in sandy areas is a shallow pit fire. Scrape a depression several inches deep in a dry streambed, sandbar, or beach—anyplace with exposed soil that contains no decomposing organic material (mineral soil)—and build your fire in the depression. Never excavate a fire pit in vegetation. Research has shown that fire pits dug in sod are still evident years later. Avoid environmental damage by using stoves and existing fire rings.

A platform or mound of mineral soil can also be used for a Leave No Trace fire. Simply pile up mineral soil into a flat-topped platform 6 to 8 inches thick and about 2 feet across and build your fire on top. The platform insulates the ground and prevents scarring. Where do you find mineral soil? Uprooted trees, sandy areas near streambeds, or exposed soil near boulder areas are all excellent sources. A tarp or fire cloth laid under the soil facilitates cleanup. Finally, portable fire pans, such as metal oil-drain pans or backyard barbecue grills, allow you to enjoy small fires with virtually no impact. The pan should be lined with mineral soil or propped up on small rocks to protect the surface underneath from heat.

The best firewood is small in diameter (1 to 2 inches), lying loose on the ground, and *not* attached to downed or standing timber. Small-diameter wood is easier to burn to ash and is less critical to the ecosystem. Gather wood from a wide area; do not denude the immediate surroundings. Collect only enough for a small fire.

Be sure to allow yourself enough time for thorough cleanup and camouflaging of the site. Regardless of whether you used an established fire ring or constructed a fire in a pristine area, burn all the wood down to cold ash. Crush any remaining charcoal. If the ash is cool enough to sift your fingers through, your fire is out. Scatter the remains and any leftover firewood far from the site.

If you constructed a mound fire, after scattering the leftover ash and small bits of charcoal, return the soil to where you found it. If the mound was built on a rock, rinse the rock off. When using a shallow pit, disperse the ash and fill in the

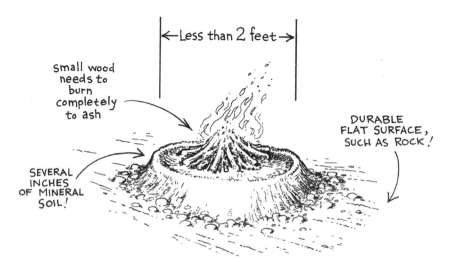

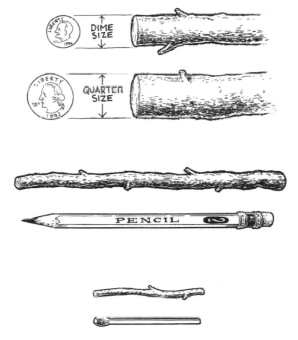

The best widths and lengths of wood to use for a cooking fire

pit with the excavated soil. Finally, camouflage the area to match the surroundings. This allows others to enjoy the same site later. Leaving no trace means leaving your cook site as clean as you found it (or cleaner) for the benefit of future campers.

Baking

You can use coals from your campfire to create a backcountry Dutch oven for baking. Set a baking pan on a flat bed of coals, and shovel coals onto the lid in an even layer for even cooking. The coals should feel very hot but not quite burn when you hold your hand 6 inches away for 8 seconds. They can be cooled by spreading them out or sprinkling them with sand. The coals on the top should be hotter than those on the bottom. Replenish coals as they go dead.

Be careful when you check the progress of your baked goods. It's safest to scrape all the coals off the lid before you peek. Don't peek too often (unless you smell burning), because the escaped heat cuts efficiency. Always wear an expendable pair of gloves—or better yet, a pair of oven mitts—when baking over an open fire.

It is also possible to bake on the stove. A great way to do this is to use a low flame under the baking pan and build a small fire with twigs on the lid. This is called a "twiggy" fire and demands a similar level of care as a larger fire (regulations, wind, wood replenishment, and so forth). For this method to work, you need a baking pan with a flat lid and no plastic parts. Bake slowly over a very low flame (offset the pan so that more than just the center gets heat), rotating the pan every few minutes to cook evenly. You can balance the pan on a flat rock to cook the outside edges. Another technique is to flip bake. This method works best with stiff breads and cakes and when you have a fairly heavy-gauge lid for the baking pan. Make sure you grease and flour the pan thoroughly, including the inside of the lid. When the dough is firm and cooked most of the way through, loosen the edges with a spatula and then flip the bread or cake onto the lid. Place the lid directly on the stove to finish cooking the top. You can also flip the entire

Use a rock to balance your pan in order to cook around the edges.

baked good in the pan to cook both sides. This works especially well with biscuits, bread, or brownies.

Other baking tips:

- Fill the pan only half full, since baked goods rise.
- The best backcountry baking pans are lightweight, have nonstick surfaces, and are of a relatively heavy gauge to distribute the often intense heat of fires and portable stoves.
- The pan should never be filled to the point that ingredients touch the lid, or they'll burn.
- Rotate the pan every few minutes to ensure even baking. This is called the "round the clock" method.
- You can use a foam sleeping pad for rolling dough. Cover it with a clean plastic bag and dust the bag with flour to prevent sticking. Improvise a rolling pin from a water bottle or a fishing rod case wrapped in clean plastic bags.

BASIC COOKING TERMINOLOGY

- *Bring to a boil:* heat a liquid until it starts to bubble over the entire surface.
- *Cream:* mix sugar and margarine or butter together until they are totally integrated and light and fluffy in texture.
- *Cooking "round the clock":* a rotation method of cooking, moving the pan "around the clock" to be sure that all areas cook thoroughly.
- *Cut in:* add margarine or butter to a mixture of dry ingredients by using two knives or two spoons, slicing the margarine in opposite directions. End result is pea-sized bits of flour-covered margarine.
- *Dice:* cut up into small cubes.
- *Fry:* cook fairly quickly in hot oil or grease in a pan, generally turning food halfway through cooking time. Food should be brown in color, but not burnt.

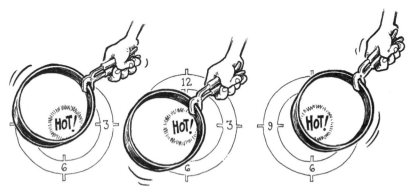

The round the clock cooking technique

- *Let rise:* allow a yeast combined with flour to double in size.
- *Parts:* an indication of proportions. For example, one part macaroni to two parts water means that whatever amount of macaroni you use, double the water—2 cups macaroni and 4 cups water.
- *Poaching:* cooking or steaming in simmering water.
- *Presoaking:* another name for rehydrating, used especially with hash browns and legumes. Presoaking cuts down on cooking time but can take 2 hours to overnight. Using hot water to start shortens presoaking time.
- *Rehydrate:* restore water to a dried food. Generally, hot water works best and fastest. In most cases, rehydration takes about 15 minutes.
- *Sauté:* similar to frying, but uses less oil and involves stirring the food as it cooks.
- *Simmer:* cook on low heat without boiling, with only occasional bubbles on the surface.
- *Twiggy fire:* a small fire built with twigs on the lid of a baking pan.

The twiggy fire

COOKING HINTS FOR BEGINNERS

"What is it, and how do I cook it quickly?" is the most common question students ask their instructors on NOLS courses. Listed below are some of the most common pitfalls for beginning cooks.

What is it?
At NOLS, where thousands of pounds of food are bagged daily, we don't mark the contents. If you're in doubt, smell it, put a little in your bowl and taste it, or ask your companions. This helps avoid mistakes such as pouring cheesecake into macaroni or pouring potato pearls into cocoa, thinking that you're adding milk. These mistakes are common and can ruin a meal.

You become more familiar with the rations after the first few days, and it gets easier to identify foods by the way they look, smell, and feel. It is the white items such as milk, cheesecake, flour, and potato pearls that can get you into trouble, so remember to identify before you mix!

- *Powdered milk:* tastes sweet, squeaks when you squeeze the bag, is lighter in color than potato pearls.
- *White flour:* tastes like paste, is very fine, and squishes to the touch.
- *Cheesecake:* squeaks when you squeeze the bag, is fine in consistency, and smells very aromatic.
- *Potato pearls:* squeak when the bag is squeezed, taste salty, smell buttery, and are more yellow in color than milk.

How do I cook it?

Use the stove carefully so as not to burn your meals. The light-weight cook pots NOLS issues are very thin on the bottom and transmit heat quite rapidly. It is imperative that you sit and monitor your cooking meal at all times. Just 2 minutes on high heat is all it takes to burn a meal. Keep in mind that no matter how much you season a burnt meal, it still tastes burnt.

A general rule is to bring the water to a boil, add the contents, and stir. Turn the heat on low, cover, and simmer, checking frequently by sticking a clean spoon down the middle of the contents to see the bottom of the pan. Usually if you smell something burning, it's too late.

Another way to avoid burning foods, especially eggs or cheese sauce, is to use pots like a double boiler: put one pot on the stove with a few inches of boiling water and set the other pot inside it.

How much seasoning should I use?

Seasoning is largely a matter of taste, not an exact science. Some guidelines:

- Never pour seasoning directly into the pot. Pour it into the cap of the spice bottle or into the stirring spoon first.
- Start with a little, taste, and add some more.
- Take into account the fact that the flavor will intensify with cooking. After seasoning, allow food to cook about 10 minutes and taste again before adding more.
- Another option is to have everyone season his or her own portion to taste.

How much should I make?

On average, a recipe requiring 1 pound of dry food (pasta, grain, beans, and so forth) feeds three people, depending on individual appetites and what else is on the menu.

What else should I know?

- Always start with a clean pot to avoid burning old food stuck on the bottom.
- A bland, "soapy" taste is most often due to a lack of salt. Salt brings out the flavor in everything, but don't overdo it. Taste first—the flavor bases already have a lot of salt in them.
- Overcooking is usually caused by poor estimation of the different cooking times of different ingredients. Add freeze-dried food to cold water, boil 10 to 15 minutes, then add rice or pasta. Thickeners (flour, potato pearls, milk, cheese) should be added just before the dish is done to avoid scorching.
- Plan ahead. If you're cook of the day, start planning dinner early in the day while you're on the trail. Have a mental agenda of what needs to be done.
- When you get to camp, boil water for hot drinks while you assemble ingredients. Assign food preparation tasks to your tentmates. Use your time and fuel efficiently.
- Tired, cold, and hungry cooks are the most likely to make mistakes. (And tired, cold, and hungry tentmates are the least forgiving.)

What if I have too much?

- *Dried fruit and nuts.* Chop them and add to hot cereals, pancakes, cookies, cakes, or rice dishes.
- *Bases—beef, chicken, or vegetable.* Add them to cooking water for rice, couscous, bulgur, or pasta; make gravies; add to boiling water for a quick hot drink.
- *Potato pearls.* Try making potato and cheese patties, or use as a thickener for soups and casseroles.
- *Couscous or bulgur.* Add it to macaroni or rice to stretch them, or try the Tabouli Salad recipe.

- *Oatmeal.* Make granola, oatmeal bread, cookies, or cake; use as a topping for fruit crisp; use in the Oat Scones recipe or for dumplings; try the recipes for the various no-bake cookies.
- *Sunflower seeds.* Add to baked goods, granola, hot cereal, or casseroles, or try dry-roasting them and sprinkling with hot sauce or cayenne.
- *Cheese.* Fry thin slices in an oiled pan; make Cheese Bombs or Cheese Carumba; serve with Oat Scones as a trail food; crumble into soups, potatoes, pastas; make nachos; eat a piece before bed to stay warm in winter.
- *Flour.* See baking and dessert recipes (many do not require twiggy fires); make pancakes, biscuits, dumplings, or tortillas.
- *Cornmeal.* Make polenta, corn tortillas, vegetarian meat-balls, cornmeal cookies, or cornmeal pancakes.
- *Margarine.* Add it to hot drinks in cold weather; make cookies; stir into hot cereals; add to grain dishes.
- *Powdered eggs.* Make quiche, an omelet, or Phil's Power Dinner; add it to baking.
- *Powdered milk.* Add it to baked goods, hot drinks, cereals, casseroles, or cream soups; try Phil's Power Dinner recipe or some hot milk drinks. Make your cocoa supply go twice as far by mixing one part cocoa with one part powdered milk and storing it in a plastic bag ready for use.

ENVIRONMENTAL CONSIDERATIONS

As an increasing number of people head into the outdoors, our impact on both the land and one another has also increased. Signs of this impact are everywhere: litter, fire scars, trampled campsites, and habituated animals are all indicators of human disturbance of wildlands. Techniques designed to minimize the social and environmental impact of backcountry visitors have been developed by the national Leave No Trace education program. These methods are summarized as the following Leave No Trace principles:

- Plan ahead and prepare.
- Camp and travel on durable surfaces.
- Pack it in, pack it out.
- Properly dispose of what you can't pack out.
- Leave what you find.
- Minimize use and impact of fires.

These principles are recommended as a guide to minimizing signs of your visit when venturing into the backcountry. For more information or written materials, call the Leave No Trace office at 1-800-332-4100, or visit their web site at http://www.lnt.org.

Kitchen Cleanup

Leaving no trace in the kitchen starts before you leave town. Part of planning ahead and preparing involves repackaging your food to minimize potential litter as well as to lighten your load. With proper meal planning and careful cooking (no burning), you can eliminate most leftovers. But if you do end

up with extra cooked food, use discretion and eat it at another
meal or carry it out. Burning leftovers requires an exception-
ally hot fire and usually results in a mess. Trash has no place
in the backcountry. Pack out what you packed in.

Certain waste—including waste water from cooking and
washing—cannot be packed out. This water should be scat-
tered widely, at least 200 feet away from any water source and
far away from campsites. Remove all food particles from the
water before disposing of it (a small strainer is good for this),
and pack them out with your trash. One exception to this is
fish guts. Fish viscera are a natural part of the ecosystem, but
disposed of improperly, they are unsightly. Disperse them
widely out of sight and well away from campsites. Don't
throw remains into high alpine lakes and streams—they
won't decompose in the cold water.

At NOLS, we use soap only for washing hands before
food preparation. We clean the dishes with nature's scrub
brushes—sand, pinecones, snow, pine needles, and bunches of

*Natural scrubbers for cleaning can be pinecones, pine needles, sand,
or snow.*

grass—and give them a good rinse with boiling water just prior to eating. With this method, no soapy dishwater is added to the environment, and it also avoids stomach upsets caused by soap residue on the dishes. However, if you want to use soap, carry a small bottle of biodegradable soap and use a few drops for cleaning. Do your dishes at least 200 feet away from any water source to prevent contaminating the water. Remember, even biodegradable soap is a foreign chemical in aquatic environments and should be used sparingly and far away from water sources.

Water Safety

These days, no matter how remote the area, there's a good chance that the water supply is contaminated by *Giardia lamblia,* a parasitic microorganism that can make life miserable. Symptoms don't appear for two to three weeks after ingestion but include severe nausea, vomiting, diarrhea, and loss of fluids.

Water boils at 212°F at sea level. *Giardia* and most other waterborne pathogens are killed at 140°F, so when small bubbles—or what we call "fish eyes"—appear, the water is safe to drink. As you go up in altitude, the temperature at which water boils goes down, but it does not get as low as 140°F until you reach extreme altitudes, so for most of the wildlands in the world, "fish eyes" is an adequate standard.

Pathogens are also killed in the cooking process, so you don't need to use treated water when mixing sauces or batters. Just don't lick the pan. For drinking water, most people either use a filter or treat their water with iodine. If you use a filter, be sure that the filter's pore size is no larger than 0.4 microns to ensure protection against *Giardia.*

Bear Country

When traveling in bear country, be sure to check recommended bear practices for the area. You'll need to take extra precautions in the selection of your kitchen site. The cooking

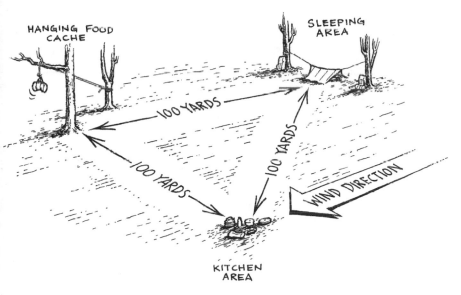

Campsite layout for bear country

area should be at least 100 yards from the sleeping area. Be sure to empty your pack of all food and odorous substances, including trail food, soap, and toothpaste, and store them in the kitchen area. Be extra careful to avoid spills on your clothing. Fish and other greasy food smells are especially attractive

Bear canisters should be used above the tree line.

to bears, so take precautions to minimize personal contact with these substances.

At night, all food and other odorous substances should be hung. If you are camping at tree level, hang food so that it's at least 12 feet above the ground at its lowest point and at least 4 feet from any part of the tree. Choose a location at least 100 yards from your sleeping area. Above the tree line, carry bear-proof canisters for food storage.

Cold Weather Conditions

It takes 15 to 20 minutes to melt snow and another 10 to 15 minutes to boil the water—half an hour before cooking can even begin. Therefore, in the winter, most food should be easy to prepare and of the one-pot meal variety. Cut foods such as cheese, salami, and bacon into bite-size pieces before your trip. Once they freeze, they become so hard to dice that you may cut yourself instead.

Obtaining water by melting snow becomes a major task (and fuel consumer) in the winter. You have to keep at it all the time, or you'll fall behind. It's easy to scorch a snow-filled pot if it's set directly on a high flame. To avoid scorching, add a little water to the bottom of the pot.

On sunny days, you can make a solar still to collect water. Place a dark-colored plastic tarp, garbage bag, or rain parka in a hollow in the snow and cover with a thin layer of snow. The sun's energy absorbed by the dark color will melt the snow. Shape a trough on one side of the tarp and drain water into a cooking pot. Large amounts of water can be obtained this way.

Because liquid intake is so important in winter (everyone should consume 3 to 4 quarts per day), bring along extra soup bases and drink mixes. Coffee and tea are diuretics, so use them in moderation in the winter. Also, it is nice to go to bed with a hot-water bottle. You can use it both for warmth and for hydration during long winter nights. Just make sure that the lid is screwed on tightly.

High Altitude

Since the time needed to boil water increases with altitude, you need to allow yourself extra cooking time. As in winter, you'll want to prepare simple one-pot meals that require little preparation or cleanup. Carbohydrates are more appealing and more easily digested than proteins or fats at high altitudes. Lighter meals are encouraged during the first three days of acclimatization, and small frequent feedings should continue for the entire time at altitude.

Fluid intake is more important than ever and should be monitored closely. Dehydration can cause acute discomfort and affect physical performance. Aim for 3 to 5 quarts per day.

recipes

BEVERAGES

COWBOY COFFEE (serves 4)

6 cups cold water
4 to 6 Tbs. ground coffee

Bring water to a boil. Add coffee and set to side of fire where it will stay hot but not boil. If using a cookstove, remove from heat and cover. Let coffee sit for a couple of minutes. Knock the side of the coffee pot with a spoon or spatula to get the grounds to settle.

Hint: A splash of cold water will help make the grounds sink but will not compromise the temperature of the coffee.

COCOA DELUXE (serves 1)

1½ cups hot water
2 Tbs. cocoa mix
1 to 2 Tbs. powdered milk
½ tsp. vanilla
dash of cinnamon

Mix cocoa mix and milk into hot water. Add vanilla and cinnamon. Stir.

Variations:

- Mocha: Make recipe above, substituting 1½ cups coffee for hot water and adding brown sugar or honey to taste.
- Cocoa Grand Deluxe: Add 1 Tbs. brown sugar and 1 Tbs. margarine for a great winter warmer.

Hint: To make your cocoa supply last longer, mix one part cocoa with one part powdered milk and store in a plastic bag ready for use.

HOT SWEET MILK (serves 1)

1½ cups hot water
2 to 3 Tbs. powdered milk
½ Tbs. honey, sugar, or molasses
½ tsp. vanilla
dash of cinnamon

Mix powdered milk and sweetener into hot water. Add vanilla and cinnamon and stir.

SUPER TEA (serves 4)

6 cups cold water
3 tea bags (Earl Grey, English Breakfast, or other black tea)
3 Tbs. lemon drink mix or 4 Tbs. orange drink mix or
    apple cider
4 whole cloves or pinch of ground cloves (optional)
pinch of cinnamon and nutmeg (optional)
3 Tbs. honey

Boil water in cooking pot. Add tea bags and steep until
desired strength. Stir in fruit drink mix, spices, and honey.

Hint: Why not place some hot water and a tea bag in one
of your water bottles at breakfast time? By midmorning, you'll
have a cool, refreshing drink.

CHAI (serves 1)

1½ cups hot water
1 tea bag (Earl Grey, English Breakfast, or other black tea)
brown sugar or honey to taste
cinnamon or nutmeg, or try mixed spices such as cloves
    and cardamom
1 to 2 Tbs. powdered milk

Steep tea bag in boiling water. Add milk, sweetener, and spices. Stir.

Variation: Add ½ Tbs. butter or margarine.

TEA VARIATIONS (serves 1)

To 1½ cups of boiling water add:
- Herbal or fruit tea bag to steep (peppermint, berry, or orange works well), then stir in 2 Tbs. cocoa mix.
- Orange spice tea bag, then add 1 Tbs. apple cider mix.
- Earl Grey, English Breakfast, or other black tea, then add 1 Tbs. either orange or lemonade drink mix.

Hint: Gelatin mix such as lemon, lime, orange, or strawberry added to boiling water makes a great alternative hot drink.

BREAKFASTS

Wouldn't Mom be happy to see you eating a good breakfast? When camping, your good breakfast can be anything from traditional breakfast foods to some creative never-before-imagined recipes of your own.

Cereals

Cereals can be eaten hot or cold. Besides hot cereals such as oatmeal and Cream of Wheat, NOLS uses a variety of cold cereals. All these cereals are versatile; they can be eaten by the handful as trail food, with cold milk, or with hot milk for a fast, hot meal.

HOT CEREALS

Instant flake-type cereals:
1 part cereal
2 parts water
salt to taste

Non-instant granular-type cereals (oatmeal, Cream of Wheat or Rice, and so forth):
1 part cereal
4 parts water
salt to taste

Boil water; add salt. Gradually pour in cereal while stirring. Stir while cooking until it reaches desired consistency, or take off heat and steam with lid on. Instant cereals take 2 to

5 minutes to cook; non-instant take 10 to 15 minutes. Add margarine, milk, sugar, fruit, and nuts in any combination to the cooked cereal.

Variation: Add cocoa, chocolate chips, or peanut butter for an action-packed hot cereal.

GRANOLA (makes 6 cups)

Good as hot or cold cereal or as a trail food.
Use quickly in hot weather.

5 Tbs. margarine
3 cups uncooked oatmeal
⅓ to ½ cup brown sugar or honey (depending on
    sweetness of fruit)
½ tsp. salt (if nuts used are unsalted)
1 cup dried fruit
1 cup nuts and seeds

Chop fruit and put into a bowl; add water to cover. Melt margarine in a frying pan. Add uncooked oatmeal and salt, stirring to coat with margarine. Sprinkle brown sugar over the top; add drained fruit and nuts. Keep stirring until oatmeal is fried to a golden brown. Can be served hot or cold.

Variation: Add ½ cup honey mixed with 2 Tbs. peanut butter.

MUESLI (makes 6 cups)

A cold cereal of oatmeal and fruit.

3 cups oatmeal
¼ cup sunflower seeds
¼ cup nuts, chopped
1 cup dried fruit, chopped
1½ cups powdered milk
2 tsp. cinnamon or a mix of spices such as cinnamon and
    nutmeg
½ tsp. salt

Mix all ingredients together in a plastic bag, ready for use. To serve, add water and stir until desired consistency is achieved; for a richer cereal, allow it to sit. This makes a very creamy cereal, naturally sweetened by the dried fruits. You can also add wheat germ, bran, or nutritional yeast for an even more nutritious breakfast.

Pancakes

SIERRA'S BAKING MIX (makes 4 ¼ cups)

This recipe makes an all-purpose Bisquick-type product that can be used, with slight variations, in many different ways. Any recipe in this book that lists "baking mix" as one of its ingredients refers to this recipe. Make up a batch and keep it in a plastic bag ready to use.

4 cups flour
2½ Tbs. baking powder
¼ cup powdered milk
2 tsp. salt

Mix all ingredients together. Store in bag until needed.

Hint: When using baking powder, never add hot or warm water. It will release its carbon dioxide, and you will end up with flat pancakes.

Ooops! I used Hot Water!

BASIC PANCAKES

2 parts baking mix (see page 63)
1 part flour or uncooked cereal
enough cold water for a pourable batter

Stir baking mix and flour or dry cereal together. Add cold water gradually until batter is a pourable consistency. Lightly grease a frying pan and heat until a few drops of water dropped in the hot pan "skitter" on the surface. Pour or spoon batter into pan and cook gently over medium heat until the bubbles on the top surface set. Flip and cook other side. Serve with margarine, peanut butter–honey spread, brown sugar–margarine syrup, or stewed fruit.

Variation: Add chopped fruit or nuts, raisins, or chocolate or carob chips to batter before cooking.

BROWN SUGAR–MARGARINE SYRUP
(makes ¼ cup)

3 Tbs. margarine
3 Tbs. brown sugar
1 tsp. vanilla

Melt margarine. Add brown sugar and heat, stirring until sugar dissolves. Remove from heat and add vanilla. Serve at once over pancakes or hot cereal. If allowed to sit, the brown sugar may harden and separate from the margarine. Reheat to reliquefy.

Variation: Add a sweet spice or combination of your choice, such as cinnamon and nutmeg.

GINGERBREAD PANCAKES
(makes 10 to 12 3-inch cakes)

1 cup baking mix (see page 63)
½ cup gingerbread mix
¾ to 1 cup cold water
1 tsp. oil or melted margarine (omit if you use a
    commercial baking mix)

Mix dry ingredients together. Add cold water gradually, stirring until mixture is thin enough to pour. Add the oil. Cook pancakes as in Basic Pancake recipe above.

DONNA'S HASH BROWN FRITTERS
(makes 8 3-inch cakes)

1 cup hash browns
1 to 2 tsp. dried onion
hot water
3 heaping Tbs. powdered milk
2 Tbs. flour
3 Tbs. powdered egg
dash of pepper
1 tsp. salt

Put hash browns and dried onions into a bowl. Cover with about 1 inch of hot water and rehydrate for 15 minutes. They should be a little firm. In another bowl, stir together dry ingredients. Drain water from potatoes, and add 6 Tbs. of potato water gradually to dry mixture, mixing well. Add this mixture to the potatoes. Drop by large spoonfuls into greased, heated frying pan. Flatten each cake. Cook about 3 minutes on each side until golden brown. Serve with brown sugar syrup, stewed fruit, or cheese and hot sauce.

RAOUL'S POTATO PANCAKES
(makes 9 to 12 6-inch cakes)

7 cups water
4 base packets, any flavor
1 heaping tsp. chili powder
1 heaping tsp. black pepper
2 heaping tsp. garlic powder
2 cups potato pearls
½ cup couscous
1½ cups flour (any kind)
⅓ pound cheese, cubed (any kind)
margarine or oil for frying

Boil water and add base packets and spices, then potatoes, couscous, and flour. Remove from heat. Stir in cheese until everything is well mixed. Cover and let sit for 10 minutes. With plastic bags on hands, shape large scoops of batter into patties and coat with flour (pat patties in flour on a plate, dip patties into plastic bag of flour, or simply scoop flour into hands and cover patties). Fry in margarine, with lid on, over medium-high heat until patties are raised, golden brown, and crispy on the outside, flipping once with a metal spatula. Let cool to solidify, and serve with salsa or ketchup on top. Makes enough for three average appetites.

Variation: Add ham or bacon bits to this recipe for a meatier version.

CORN PANCAKES
(makes 10 to 12 3-inch cakes)

1 cup cornmeal
½ cup powdered milk
½ tsp. salt
1½ cups water
2 Tbs. oil or melted margarine
1 Tbs. brown sugar

Combine cornmeal, milk, and salt. Add water, oil, and brown
sugar; mix well. Cook in hot, oiled frying pan. Good with
brown sugar, syrup, or stewed fruit.

Hint: A pan is the right temperature for cooking pancakes
when a few drops of water dropped in the hot oiled pan "skitter" on the surface.

OATMEAL HOTCAKES
(makes about 12 3-inch cakes)

2 cups oatmeal
¼ cup raisins
¼ cup mixed fruit, chopped
½ cup powdered milk
¼ tsp. cinnamon
¼ tsp. salt
1½ cups warm water

Using the butt of a spice bottle, grind the oatmeal to a flour-
like consistency, leaving some small pieces. Combine all ingredients with warm water and let soak for one hour. To cook:
Form into 3-inch cakes about ¾ inch thick and fry slowly in a
little hot oil until golden brown.

WHOLE WHEAT PANCAKES
(makes about 12 3-inch cakes)

1 cup whole wheat flour
1 cup white flour
1 heaping Tbs. powdered eggs
1 heaping Tbs. powdered milk
pinch of salt
½ tsp. cinnamon
3 heaping Tbs. margarine, melted
1 tsp. vanilla
3 cups cold water
½ tsp. baking powder

Mix all dry ingredients except baking powder together. Add melted margarine to water and slowly add to dry ingredients, stirring well to prevent lumps. Add baking powder and vanilla and stir well. Heat frying pan and add ½ Tbs. margarine. Fry cakes on both sides until golden brown. Serve with brown sugar and margarine or stewed fruit. Good cold for trail food.

Breakfast Grains

BREAKFAST COUSCOUS (serves 4)

    4 cups water
    ¼ tsp. salt
    3 Tbs. brown sugar or honey
    ¼ cup margarine
    ¼ cup dried fruit, chopped
    2 cups couscous
    2 Tbs. powdered milk mixed with 4 Tbs. water
    ½ to 1 tsp. cinnamon
    ¼ cup sunflower seeds or nuts

Bring water to a boil with salt, brown sugar, margarine, and fruit. Add couscous and milk mixture and stir. Cover and simmer for 5 to 10 minutes, stirring occasionally. When water is gone and mixture has fluffed up, mix in the cinnamon and nuts.

Variation: For Breakfast Bulgur, substitute 2 cups water and 1 cup bulgur for couscous and water; reduce sugar and margarine to 2 Tbs. each; use ½ tsp. either cinnamon or nutmeg. Optional: stir in 1 tsp. vanilla and 2 Tbs. peanut butter when done.

Hint: A 16 ounce (500 ml) plastic storage tub with a secure screw-on lid makes a great eating bowl and an excellent cooking tool.

Add dry ingredients like oatmeal, rice, or couscous to the tub, add the recommended amount of boiling water and quickly add the lid. Wait a few moments then shake vigorously! If you shake too soon, the lid will leak because of the pressure caused by expanding hot water. Next insulate the tub so the meal can cook completely without cooling too soon. Wrap the tub in a jacket or stuff it in next to your body. There's no better place for your oatmeal on a cold morning! Ready to eat in about ten minutes. Clean up is easy; add warm water, replace the lid and shake.

Use extreme caution with a Tupperware container's 'pop-on' type lid. It can burst off when the water expands.

HOT SWEET RICE (serves 1)

½ cup hot milk
½ Tbs. margarine
½ Tbs. brown sugar or honey
dash of cinnamon or nutmeg
1 cup cooked rice
2 Tbs. raisins or other fruit and/or nuts

Add the margarine, brown sugar, and cinnamon to hot milk. In a separate bowl, mix fruit and/or nuts into the rice and pour the hot milk mixture over the top. Stir and eat.

A plastic storage tub with a secure screw-on lid makes a great eating bowl

Other Breakfast Recipes

BAGELS

Bagels are a versatile food for breakfast or for a snack. They can be coated with margarine and toasted in a frying pan, or they can be spread with cream cheese, peanut butter, or honey and eaten cold.

Variations:

- Cheese bagels: Fry bagel halves facedown in 2 Tbs. margarine in a pan. Flip over and layer with cheese. Cover and cook over medium heat for 2 to 3 minutes. Sprinkle with hot sauce or spices to taste.
- Bacon bagels: Fry bacon and remove from pan. Fry bagel halves facedown in bacon fat. Flip over and layer with cheese. Cover pan and cook for 2 to 3 minutes until cheese melts. Add crumbled bacon on top. Add hot sauce or spices to taste.

HASH BROWNS WITH CHEESE (serves 2)

1½ cups hash browns
hot water
4 to 5 Tbs. margarine
1 Tbs. onion, rehydrated or fresh, finely chopped (optional)
½ cup cheese cubes or grated cheese
salt and pepper to taste

Put hash browns into a saucepan. Cover with 1 inch of hot water and rehydrate for 15 minutes. Drain off excess water. Melt margarine in a hot fry pan. Add hash browns and onions. Cook, flipping occasionally, until crisp and browned. Stir in or cover with cheese and remove from heat. Cover and allow to sit until cheese is melted. Salt and pepper to taste. Good with hot sauce or picante.

Variation: Add ham or bacon bits to hash browns and cook as above.

EGGS MCGULCH (serves 1)

2 heaping Tbs. powdered egg
1 Tbs. powdered milk
1 Tbs. flour
½ cup water
salt, pepper, and other spices to taste
margarine
1 bagel, sliced
cheese: cream, jack, or cheddar
salsa or ketchup

In a bowl, mix egg, milk, and flour together and slowly add water, stirring constantly to avoid clumping. Pour mixture into a heated fry pan, with a little bit of margarine, and stir constantly to avoid burning. Remove from heat when eggs reach a scrambled consistency. Add spices to taste. Spread margarine on bagel and toast in fry pan. Spread cream cheese, or place sliced cheese, on bagel; top with cooked eggs and salsa or ketchup. Makes one hearty breakfast sandwich.

Variations: Add fresh or rehydrated onions, green and red peppers, or cooked meat to eggs.

BASIC OMELET (serves 1)

1 heaping Tbs. powdered egg
1 heaping Tbs. powdered milk
1 heaping Tbs. baking mix (see page 63)
½ cup cold water (approximate)
1 Tbs. dried onions
1 to 2 Tbs. margarine
3 Tbs. potato pearls
⅓ cup cheese, cubed or grated (any kind will work)
1 tsp. soy sauce

In a bowl, mix dry egg, milk, and baking mix together. Add cold water gradually, stirring to keep from lumping. In a separate bowl, pour a small amount of hot water over onions and let hydrate. Melt 1 to 2 Tbs. margarine in hot frying pan. Pour in egg mixture and swirl around so it covers entire bottom of pan. Cover and cook over medium to low heat. It will set quickly. In another bowl, mix potato pearls, drained onions, and cheese with enough hot water to make a smooth mixture. Stir in the soy sauce. Spread mixture over half the omelet. Fold other side over potatoes and cook a minute to heat up. Top with more cheese, cover, and let sit until cheese is melted. Try topping this with hot sauce or picante.

Variations: Add fresh veggies, ham, or bacon bits to the potato filling.

DINNERS

Pastas

BASIC PASTA RECIPE (serves about 3)

1 part pasta (2 cups)
2 parts water (4 cups)
salt to taste

Add pasta to boiling salted water; boil gently 10 to 15 minutes. Drain water and add sauce to cooked pasta.

Note: When cooking pasta, watch it carefully, as it can quickly go from still chewy to mushy. Drain it immediately, because leaving it in the water, even if the pan is removed from the heat, continues the cooking process. Adding 1 tsp. of oil or margarine to the cooking water prevents pasta from cementing together when the water is drained.

MACS AND CHEESE (serves 3 to 4)

4 cups water
1 tsp. salt
2 Tbs. onions or other dried vegetables if desired
2 cups pasta
3 to 4 Tbs. margarine
1 cup diced cheese
4 Tbs. powdered milk
black pepper and garlic to taste

Add salt and vegetables to water. Bring to a boil. Add pasta; boil 8 to 15 minutes depending on the pasta type, stirring occasionally. Drain out any water in excess of ¼ cup. Add margarine and cheese; stir. Add enough water to powdered milk to make a thick liquid. Add it and any spices to pasta. Cook and stir until cheese is melted.

Hint: If you don't want to waste the water drained from your pasta, why not you use it for soup or a hot drink to sip while you eat your meal?

FRIED MACS (serves 2 to 4)

handful of dried vegetables
1 lb. macaroni (or any pasta)
4 to 6 cups water
fresh or dried garlic
spices to taste, such as salt, pepper, soy sauce, oregano,
    basil
oil or margarine
cheese (any kind), cubed

Add vegetables to cold water and bring to a boil. Add pasta,
bring back to a boil, remove from heat, and cover. In another
pan, sauté garlic and spices in oil or margarine and then add
cooked, drained pasta. Stir and fry for 5 to 10 minutes. Add
cubed cheese and fry until desired consistency. Top with
Parmesan or salsa for added flavor.

Variations: Use other types of pasta, but be aware that
spinach fettucine and egg noodles require constant heat while
cooking to avoid mushiness. You can also add canned meats
such as tuna or chicken or fresh meats such as pepperoni,
cooked bacon, or sausage to this meal for added flavor and
calories.

Hint: The smaller the cheese chunks, the faster the cheese
will melt.

GADO-GADO SPAGHETTI (serves 2 to 3)

*A spicy peanut butter sauce makes this a light spaghetti dish
that is excellent either hot or cold.*

½ lb. spaghetti or ramen noodles
4 cups water
3 Tbs. + 1 tsp. oil
2 Tbs. sunflower seeds
1 Tbs. dried onion, rehydrated
½ Tbs. or one packet base*
3 Tbs. brown sugar
1 tsp. garlic
½ tsp. black pepper (optional)
½ tsp. hot sauce (optional)
½ tsp. spike (optional)
¾ cup water, or more as needed
3 Tbs. vinegar
3 Tbs. soy sauce
3 Tbs. peanut butter
sliced green or wild onions, if available

Break pasta in half and put into boiling *unsalted* water to
which 1 tsp. of oil has been added. Cook until done; drain
immediately. In a fry pan, heat 3 Tbs. oil and add the sunflower seeds and rehydrated onions. Cook and stir over
medium heat for 2 minutes. Add the base with the brown
sugar, garlic, other spices if desired, and ¾ cup water. Add the
vinegar and soy sauce. Add peanut butter and stir. *Do not
burn!* To eat this hot, heat the sauce thoroughly and pour over
hot spaghetti.

This recipe is best cold, and it loses some of its saltiness as
it sits. Mix sauce and spaghetti, cool quickly, and serve chilled.
If available, sliced green or wild onions as a garnish add to the
flavor.

*This dish can have a fairly salty taste. Cut back or eliminate the base if you
are concerned about saltiness.

Variation: Fresh vegetables such as broccoli, onions, and cabbage, chopped and sautéed lightly and mixed into the sauce, make a tasty addition.

Rice

When cooking rice or grains, put a spoon into the pot, gently push the grain aside, and check the bottom to see if the water has been absorbed; do not overstir, as it will become starchy.

BASIC RICE RECIPE (serves 2)

2 cups water
½ tsp. salt
1 cup rice
½ Tbs. margarine

Add salt to water and bring to a boil. Add rice and margarine and return to boiling. Cover and reduce heat. Simmer for 20 to 30 minutes.

FRIED RICE

Cook rice as above. Melt margarine or put oil in frying pan. Add any spices such as curry, garlic, or salt and pepper. Fry rice until golden brown, 10 to 15 minutes. Do not overload pan, as it increases frying time.

RICE CASSEROLES

All casserole recipes under Pastas can be made by substituting rice for the pasta.

SWEET AND SOUR RICE (serves 3 to 4)

2 ½ cups water
1 cup rice
1 tsp. salt
½ cup raisins
½ cup other dried fruit, chopped
2 Tbs. dried green and red peppers
2 Tbs. dried onion (optional)
½ cup nuts and seeds
1 to 2 Tbs. curry powder
¼ tsp. black pepper
2 Tbs. margarine

Sauce:
¼ cup water
4 Tbs. vinegar (omitting removes "sour" element, but
    results are still good)
3 Tbs. soy sauce
3 to 5 Tbs. brown sugar or 3 to 4 Tbs. honey

Put water, rice, salt, raisins, peppers, dried fruit, and dried onion into a pan. Cook, covered, until rice is done. Drain if necessary. Add nuts and spices and fry in margarine 5 to 10 minutes.

For sauce, mix water, vinegar, soy sauce, and brown sugar together. Stir thoroughly into rice. Simmer a few minutes with the cover on. Serve.

Variations: Use ½ cup rice and ½ cup bulgur. Add 1 to 2 Tbs. curry powder when making for Sweet and Sour Curried Rice.

GRAIN NUT LOAF (makes 1 loaf)

This was a hit with our tasters when served either hot or cold.

1½ cups cooked white or brown rice, bulgur, or couscous
¾ cup chopped nuts (walnuts work best)
¼ cup chopped sunflower seeds
1 Tbs. dried onion, rehydrated in hot water
1 cup shredded or small-diced cheese (cheddar and jack
  are good)
½ cup flour
½ tsp. salt
4 Tbs. powdered eggs
6 Tbs. water (approximate)

Mix all ingredients together, adding water last in an amount
that will moisten all the ingredients just enough to hold them
together. Form a round loaf about 1 inch thick and place in
the center of an oiled fry pan (or use an 8- or 9-inch loaf pan).
Cover and bake over medium heat for 30 to 50 minutes. Let sit
10 minutes before slicing. Good hot or cold, plain or with a
flavored white sauce.

SPANISH RICE WITH BEANS (serves 3) NEW!

½ cup white rice, presoaked
½ cup pinto beans, presoaked
3 to 4½ cups water
2 Tbs. dried green and red pepper
1 Tbs. dried onion
¼ to ½ tsp. cumin (optional)
½ tsp. salt
1 tsp. garlic powder
2 heaping Tbs. tomato base
2 Tbs. chili powder
1 cup cheese, cubed

Start with 3 cups water and add more if necessary. Put all ingredients, except cheese, together in a pot. Cover and bring to a boil. Cook 20 to 30 minutes, until rice and beans are soft and most of the water is absorbed, stirring often to prevent burning. Turn off heat, add cheese, and cover for a few minutes to let cheese melt. Great with tortillas.

Variation: If using instant refried beans instead of whole beans, add rice and all other ingredients except beans and cheese to 1½ cups water. Cook as directed. Add 1 cup instant refried beans to 2 cups water and cook until thick. Stir into the rice mixture when you add the cheese.

RICE IN NUT CURRY SAUCE (serves 2)

1 cup rice
1 Tbs. margarine
2 to 3 Tbs. dried peas and carrots or mixed vegetables
1 Tbs. dried onion
2 tsp. curry
½ Tbs. or 1 packet base
¼ tsp. garlic
2 cups water
1 tsp. soy sauce
1 tsp. vinegar (optional)

Sauce:
1 cup white sauce made without salt (see page 108)
1 tsp. brown sugar
2 Tbs. raisins or other chopped dried fruits
2 Tbs. chopped almonds or other nuts
½ to 1 tsp. curry powder
dash of cumin (optional)
2 tsp. soy sauce
cayenne or hot sauce to taste

Mix all rice ingredients except soy sauce and vinegar in a fry pan. Cover and cook until rice is done (20 to 30 minutes for regular parboiled rice). Stir in soy sauce and vinegar. Make white sauce; add all other sauce ingredients except cayenne or hot sauce; blend and cook until heated through. Mix sauce into rice or pour over individual bowls. Add cayenne or hot sauce to taste.

Variations: Add 1 can of chicken to the rice as it cooks, or add dried banana and coconut.

Hint: If the whole group likes curry, add it to both the rice and the sauce to taste. If some don't like it, omit it from the rice and let them eat the rice with soy sauce instead of curry sauce.

Grains

Couscous. Couscous is a nutritious durum wheat product common in the North African desert countries and in Europe. It fits well into the NOLS food program because it is inexpensive, tastes great, and cooks quickly. It resembles millet in color, grits in texture, and rice in its cooked state. Good for breakfast or dinner.

CLAUDIA'S FAVORITE COUSCOUS PILAF
(serves 4)

---

4 cups water
1 Tbs. or 1 to 2 packets base
2 to 4 Tbs. dried vegetables (peas and carrots are good)
2 cups dry couscous
4 Tbs. margarine (or more to taste)
1 to 2 cups finely cubed cheddar or jack cheese

Bring water, base , and dried vegetables to a rolling boil. Add couscous and margarine. Stir well; cover and cook on low for 10 to 15 minutes. Check frequently, as it can burn easily. Once grain looks dry and light, remove from heat. Stir in cheese; cover for a few minutes until cheese is melted. Serve with soy or hot sauce.

Note: Margarine is the key ingredient to success in this recipe.

Bulgur. Bulgur is cracked wheat that has been parboiled, then dried. Bulgur is a versatile food that cooks quickly and can be eaten as a breakfast cereal or a dinner food like rice or couscous, or it can be added to bread and pancakes in place of part of the flour. The ratio of bulgur to water for cooking is 1 part bulgur to 2 parts water (same as for rice or couscous).

BULGUR-RICE PILAF (serves 3 to 4)

1 cup bulgur
1 cup rice
4 cups water (seasoned with any base to taste)
2 Tbs. dried mixed vegetables
1 Tbs. dried onion
3 heaping Tbs. margarine
½ cup cubed cheese

Add all ingredients except cheese to a pot. Cook, covered, over medium heat for 20 minutes. Stir as little as possible. When dry and fluffy, add cheese and scoop into oiled fry pan; fry until browned.

TABOULI SALAD

Great as a side dish or as a sandwich filler.

2 cups bulgur
2½ cups boiling water
1 Tbs. dried onion
2 to 3 Tbs. dried mixed vegetables
1 mint tea bag
2 Tbs. parsley flakes
½ cup oil
1 tsp. salt
¼ to ½ tsp. pepper
5 Tbs. lemon juice (optional; vinegar may also be used)

Place bulgur, 2 cups boiling water, dried onion, and dried vegetables in a pot. Steep tea bag in remaining ½ cup water for 2 to 3 minutes. Discard tea bag and add water to bulgur. Let sit for ½ hour. Add remaining ingredients. Stir well. Allow to sit another ½ hour before eating.

Polenta. Polenta is a special Italian grind of corn. Corn-meal works well as a substitute. It cooks up thick and can be eaten sweet or spicy.

BASIC POLENTA RECIPE (serves 3 to 4)

1 cup cornmeal
1 tsp. salt
3 to 4 cups water (4 if you want it as a hot cereal, 3 if you
    want it firmer for fried cakes)
2 Tbs. margarine (optional)

Mix cornmeal and salt in a pan. Add water gradually, stirring to prevent lumps. Bring to a boil, then reduce heat and simmer 5 to 10 minutes, stirring often. Be careful cooking this, as it can spew out hot cornmeal lava bombs if the heat is too high. Stir in margarine. To serve, add raisins or other fruit, brown sugar or honey, and nuts. Or try Parmesan or crumbled cheddar, sunflower seeds, and hot sauce.

FRIED POLENTA CAKES

Let cooked polenta cool for a while to thicken, then form into cakes or cut into slices. Fry on both sides in margarine in a hot pan. Serve plain or with honey.

Variations:

- Fry on one side, turn, spread top with a sauce made of 1 part tomato base to 2 parts water, and sprinkle with crumbled cheese; continue cooking until cheese melts.
- Mix 2 Tbs. powdered eggs with 3 Tbs. water. Pat onto cakes and then roll them in either a cornmeal and flour mix or ground-up oatmeal or wheat germ with salt and pepper. Fry until brown, turning once.
- Serve cooked cakes with a white sauce flavored with garlic and cheese.

Falafel. Falafel is a Middle Eastern staple made of ground chickpeas (garbanzo beans), yellow peas, whole wheat flour, onion, baking powder, and spices. Because it can be rather dry, it is best served with a sauce or, if car camping, in pita bread with lettuce, tomato, cucumber, and plain yogurt or tahini sauce.

BASIC FALAFEL RECIPE (serves 2 to 3)

1 cup falafel mix
¾ cup water
oil for frying

Stir water thoroughly into mix and allow to sit 10 minutes.
Shape into small patties and fry on both sides in hot oil
to desired crispness. Serve with rice or pasta and a seasoned
white sauce or gravy (see sauce recipes, page 108). Also good
with cheese melted on top.
    Variation: For a milder version, mix half falafel with half
cornmeal or flour.

Potatoes

BASIC POTATO RECIPE (serves 1)

⅓ cup potato pearls
⅔ to 1 cup boiling water
margarine to taste

Put pearls in a bowl. Add boiling water gradually until potatoes reach desired consistency. Stir in margarine.
    Variations: Stir in grated or chunked cheese. Make pota-
toes with less water, form into patties, and fry in margarine.
After turning, add slice of cheese to top and allow to melt.
Good with hot sauce or picante.

    Hint: Add potato pearls to soup with cheese for a quick
and easy one-cup meal. Potato pearls also make great thickeners in just about everything except cocoa.

POTATO-CHEESE PATTIES
(makes 12 3-inch cakes)

2 cups water
2 Tbs. dried onion
1 cup potato pearls
½ to 1 cup powdered milk, dry
½ cup baking mix (see page 63)
2 Tbs. dried mixed vegetables (optional)
pepper to taste
¼ cup flour or cornmeal
margarine for frying

Boil water with onions and vegetables. Add to potato pearls
and stir well. Cool for about 5 minutes. Mix in all other ingredients except flour or cornmeal and margarine; Form a stiff
dough. Shape dough into patties and roll them in the flour or
cornmeal. Fry in margarine until both sides are slightly
crisped. Good with picante or hot sauce or, if you're adventur-
ous, with peanut butter.

Variation: Add ½ cup sunflower seeds or chopped nuts to
the mixture before cooking.

Hint: Shape patties while wearing two plastic bags on
your hands.

 TARTER'S TASTY TATERS (serves 3 to 4)

½ lb. potato pearls
black pepper, salt, garlic powder, hot sauce, chili powder
¾ lb. refried beans or instant black beans
3 Tbs. margarine
⅓ lb. Grapenuts
¾ lb. cheddar cheese

Boil 8 cups water. Use enough of it to hydrate potato pearls in a pot, spicing to taste with pepper, salt, garlic, hot sauce, and chili powder. Then use leftover water to cook beans. In fry pan, melt margarine and add ⅔ of the Grapenuts. Fry until coated with margarine and then pat into a crust on the bottom of the fry pan. Cover the crust with a layer of sliced cheddar. Scoop in potato pearls and flatten on top of crust. Pour beans on top of the layer of pearls. Cover beans with a layer of cheddar cheese. Sprinkle the remaining Grapenuts on top of the cheese and sprinkle everything with a dash of chili powder for color. Bake the casserole until the cheese on top has started to melt and bubble (about 10 to 15 minutes). It is safest to put the fry pan on top of the Whisper Lite windscreen so as not to burn the bottom layer of Grapenuts.

Beans and Legumes
The following recipes use instant refried or black beans.

SPICY BEANS AND MACS (serves 4)

2 cups refried beans
5+ cups water
1 Tbs. dried onion
2 to 4 Tbs. dried green and red peppers
salt, black pepper, garlic, oregano, chili powder to taste
1 Tbs. base or miso, or 1 vegetable bouillon cube or base
    packet
1 Tbs. margarine
2 to 3 cups pasta (other than spaghetti)
cheddar or jack cheese

Add all ingredients except pasta and cheese to water. Cook until beans are tender. Mixture should be brothy, so add more hot water if needed. Cooking time depends on elevation. When beans are nearly done (gravylike consistency), cook pasta separately. Drain it and stir into the beans. Add grated cheese and salsa to individual portions.

REFRIED BEANS AND TORTILLAS
(serves 2 to 3)

3 cups water
1 Tbs. dried onion
3 Tbs. tomato base
3 Tbs. powdered milk
1½ cups instant refried or black beans
chili powder, salt, pepper, and cumin to taste
cheese cubes
2 heaping Tbs. margarine
tortillas (commercial or see page 123)
1 small can chopped green chilies (optional)

Put water and dried onion in a large pan, and bring to a boil.
Put the tomato and milk powders into a cup, and add some of
the water slowly, stirring to prevent lumps. Add the rest of the
water to the beans, and stir until water is absorbed. Stir the
tomato and milk mixture into the beans. Add seasonings and
chilies. When beans are done, you can add cheese, cover, and
set aside, or add cheese later as you make up the individual
servings. Fry tortillas on both sides in small amount of margarine or oil; the longer you fry them, the crispier they get. Spoon
beans onto tortillas. Add sunflower seeds or cooked red and
green peppers if desired; sprinkle with hot sauce or picante.

LENTIL CHILI (serves 2 to 3)

1 cup lentils, presoaked, or instant lentils
3 Tbs. tomato base
2 Tbs. cornmeal (optional)
1 Tbs. chili powder
1 Tbs. dried onion
1 tsp. oregano
1 tsp. garlic powder
4 cups water
1½ cup cheese cubes

Combine all ingredients except cheese. Bring to a boil; cover and reduce heat to medium. Simmer for about 30 minutes until lentils are soft. Fill individual bowls and top with cheese.

Hint: If using instant lentils, there is no need to presoak, and adjustments may need to be made in the amount of spices used if the lentils are preflavored, such as the instant curried lentils issued by NOLS.

LENTIL CASSEROLE (serves 3 to 4)

1 cup lentils, presoaked, or instant lentils
½ to 1 tsp. salt (optional)
1 cup potato pearls
soy sauce to taste
½ to 1 cup cheese

Pour presoaked lentils into a pan. Add water to cover lentils; then add one more inch of water. Stir in salt. Bring to boiling; cover and reduce heat. Cook at a slow boil for 15 to 30 minutes, until lentils are soft (or until rehydrated for instant lentils). Drain off juice and keep it. Use some of the juice to mix up the instant potatoes, adding soy sauce to taste. In a frying pan, spread the potatoes in a layer, and cover with the lentils. Top with crumbled or sliced cheese. Pour some of the lentil juice over the top to moisten the casserole. You can sprinkle the top with sunflower seeds or Grapenuts if desired. Cover and bake until cheese is melted and casserole is heated through. Good with NOLS picante (see page 109).

LENTIL RICE CAKES (makes 8 3-inch cakes)

⅔ cup white rice
½ cup lentils, presoaked, or instant lentils
2 cups water
1 tsp. salt
1 Tbs. dried onion
¼ tsp. oregano
dash of garlic
soy sauce to taste
1 to 2 Tbs. white flour
margarine for frying

Put rice, lentils, water, salt, and onions into a pot. Cook, covered, until lentils are soft, about 20 to 30 minutes (or until rehydrated, if using instant lentils). Stir in spices and soy sauce. Mash with spoon. Stir in flour to help hold mixture together. Form into patties. Fry in margarine until both sides are slightly crisped. Great with picante, spicy peanut sauce, or a flavored white sauce.

Variation: These lentil recipes are great made with brown rice, but it takes much longer to cook.

Fish

Fish may be cleaned and cooked whole if small. If large or thick, they can be cut into ½- to 1-inch steaks or fillets. To fillet, hold fish by the tail and slice toward the head, cutting the meat off where it joins the bone. When one side is done, do the other.

Filleting a Fish

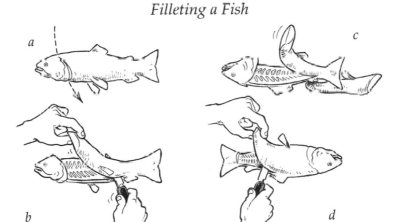

a. Make a cut to the bone at the fish's gill, taking care not to puncture the internal organs. Do not cut off the head. b. Cut down along the backbone, starting at the head and moving toward the tail. Leave the fillet attached to the tail. c. Turn the fish over and repeat the same procedure on the second side. d. The fillet cut can also be done by starting at the tail and cutting toward the head.

Hint: It's best not to put freshly caught fish in a plastic bag, because it can get too warm. The fats turn to oils, and the flesh takes on a fishy aroma and taste.

Gutting a Fish

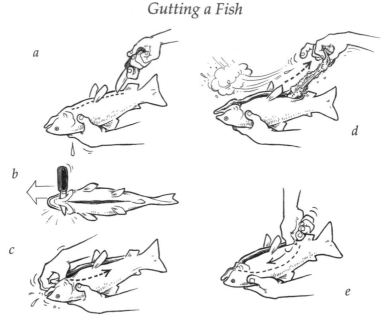

a. Make a shallow cut, beginning at the vent of the fish and running along the stomach to the throat. Be careful not to puncture the innards. b. Make a horizontal cut through the throat, just below the lower jaw. c. Grasp the open flap at the throat created by the horizontal cut. d. Pull out the innards along the shallow cut. e. Clean any remaining blood or material out of the bloodline.

FRIED FISH (serves 1)

---

1 cleaned fish, slightly wet, either whole or cut into steaks
   or fillets
¼ to ½ cup cornmeal (white or wheat flour can also be
   used)
½ tsp. salt
black pepper, garlic powder, dill, dry mustard, or curry to
   taste
oil or margarine for frying (oil gives better taste and
   crispness)

Mix cornmeal or flour, salt, and any desired spices in a plastic bag. Put in slightly wet fish and shake to coat. Remove fish and place it in hot oil or melted margarine in a frying pan. Fry slowly until fish is tender and flakes apart. Several cuts on the back of a whole fish or turning the fish frequently can prevent it from curling as it cooks.

Variation: Mix 1 Tbs. powdered egg with 2 to 3 Tbs. water and dip fish in this before coating with cornmeal or flour.

BAKED FISH (serves 1)

Throw a whole, cleaned fish directly on hot coals. Turn when done on first side and continue cooking. Take off coals and season with salt and pepper to taste.

Variation: Steaks or fillets can be sprinkled with seasoning on both sides and added to melted margarine in a covered fry pan. Bake for about 20 to 25 minutes or until fish flakes apart.

BONED FISH

If you need just the meat, boil the cleaned fish, head and all, for 10 to 15 minutes until the meat starts to fall off the bone. Remove fish from water and strip off meat with a knife or fingers. Discard bones but save water for stock.

CREAMED FISH

Pour a white sauce made with vegetables and spices over fish that has been boiled, poached, or baked.

Variations: A creamy tomato sauce with onions, spiced cheese sauce, or white sauce with dill or mustard are good combinations.

FISH PATTIES (serves about 3)

fish, boiled or poached and then boned
fish stock
1 to 2 Tbs. dried onion, boiled with fish
1½ cups potato pearls
⅓ to ½ cup dry powdered milk
salt and pepper to taste
margarine for frying

Cook fish in fish stock with onions. Remove fish from stock, bone, and flake the meat into little pieces. To potato pearls, dry milk, and salt and pepper, add enough of the fish stock to make a mashed potato consistency. Add flaked fish to this and mix well. Form into thick patties and fry on both sides in melted margarine until golden brown. Serve with a white, cheese, or dill sauce.

FISH-POTATO CASSEROLE (serves 3 to 4)

2 cups dried potato slices or hash browns
2 Tbs. dried onion
2 to 3 cups white sauce seasoned with salt and pepper to
    taste (the moister the casserole, the better)
3 Tbs. margarine
1 to 2 cups boned fish

Put potatoes and onions in a large pot; cover with 1 inch of hot water and rehydrate for 15 minutes. Drain water and use it to make the white sauce. Melt 1 Tbs. margarine in frying pan. Add layer of drained potatoes, layer of flaked fish, layer of white sauce. Repeat. Dot top with remaining margarine. Sprinkle with Grapenuts or sunflower seeds if desired. Cover pan and cook on medium heat for 20 to 25 minutes, using the round the clock method of rotating the pan until potatoes are cooked and casserole is bubbly.

FISH CHOWDER (serves 3 to 4)

Fish, cleaned
4 Tbs. dried onion
4 Tbs. other dried vegetables
8 cups water
salt and pepper to taste
½ cup margarine

Cook fish in water with onions and vegetables until fish is
ready to bone (about 10 to 15 minutes). Remove fish, bone it,
and return fish to stock. Spice to taste. Add margarine.
Reduce heat to simmer.

Variations: For New England style, add ¾ cup potato
pearls and ⅔ cup dry powdered milk; heat through and serve.
For Manhattan style, add 3 to 4 Tbs. tomato base, ½ cup dry
powdered milk (optional), and ¼ to ½ tsp. oregano; heat
through and serve.

Specialties of the House

PHIL'S POWER DINNER (serves 4)

2 cups bulgur or couscous
4+ cups water
1 tsp. salt (divided)
1 to 2 Tbs. dried peas and carrots
2 Tbs. margarine
½ to 1 cup grated or cubed cheese (optional)
4 to 6 Tbs. powdered eggs
¾ cup powdered milk
4 Tbs. flour
1 tsp. baking powder
½ tsp. garlic powder
¼ tsp. black pepper

Cook bulgur or couscous in 4 cups water to which ½ tsp. salt and dried vegetables have been added. When done, stir in margarine and cheese. Pour into a fry pan. In a bowl, mix eggs, milk, flour, baking powder, ½ tsp. salt, garlic, and pepper. Mix well. Gradually add enough water to make a sauce consistency (not a paste). Pour this over grain in fry pan, cover tightly, and cook over medium heat, using round the clock method of rotation. Dish is done when topping is set and cooked through, about 20 to 30 minutes. Serve with soy sauce, Tabasco, or picante.

 ## MEXICAN CORNMEAL PIE (serves 3 to 4)

Bean filling:
2 cups refried or black beans
2 to 3 tsp. cumin
2 to 3 tsp. garlic
1 tsp. salt
2 to 3 tsp. chili powder

Cornbread:
1½ cups flour
1½ cups cornmeal
2 tsp. baking powder
dash salt
3 Tbs. brown sugar or honey
dash oil
water

To make the filling, hydrate the beans in boiled water for 10 minutes. Add any or all of the spices to taste. To make the cornbread, mix dry ingredients and then add brown sugar, oil, and enough cold water to make a thick batter that still pours. Grease and flour fry pan. Pour half of cornbread mixture into pan. Spread bean filling over cornbread batter. Layer the remaining cornbread over the beans. Cover and bake with a twiggy fire on top over moderate heat. Be careful not to burn the bottom. Bake using the round the clock method for 30 to 40 minutes, or until cornbread on top is golden brown. Sprinkle grated cheese on top and let melt, or layer cheese on top of bean filling before adding remaining cornmeal batter on top.

Variations: Add a layer of salsa on the bean filling in the pie itself, or simply top with salsa. You can add green chilies, leftover rice, and cheese to the bean mixture for a heartier meal.

PIZZA AND CALZONES (serves 1 to 2)

Yeast crust (preferred):
1 tsp. dry yeast
½ cup lukewarm water
½ tsp. sugar
¼ tsp. salt
1 cup flour
OR
Quick crust (flakier):
½ cup baking mix (see page 63)
½ cup flour
1 Tbs. margarine

Sauce:
spaghetti sauce, white sauce with tomato base, or Mexican
    sauce (see pages 110, 108, 111)

Possible toppings:
fish; wild onions; bacon or ham bits; ham or sausage; jack,
    cheddar, or mozzarella cheese crumbled or thinly
    sliced

For yeast crust, dissolve yeast in warm water with sugar and salt. Add flour and mix to make a stiff dough. For quick crust, mix margarine into flour and baking mix with fingers. Mix in water to form a dough. Oil a fry pan, and spread dough in pan with oiled fingers to form a crust. Turn up edges to hold sauce. Pour sauce over crust, and top with cheese and any other toppings. Cover and bake on a stove on low heat until crust is golden brown, about 20 to 25 minutes. Or you can use a twiggy fire, which helps cook crust from both top and bottom. Be sure to move the pan in round the clock rotation in quarter turns to bake all parts of the pizza.

Alternative cooking method: Put crust in pan and cook for about 10 minutes; flip, spread with sauce and cheese, cover, and continue cooking for another 10 minutes.

Variation: For calzones, spread flattened dough in pan and cover one half with desired toppings. Fold other half of dough over the top and pinch edges together to seal in toppings. Cook about 10 minutes on each side, or use a twiggy fire and bake for about 20 minutes.

CHEESE BOMBS

½ cup flour
¼ cup baking mix (see page 63)
¼ cup powdered egg
½ to 1 Tbs. or 1 packet base
seasoning of choice*
cheddar or jack cheese

Mix all ingredients together except cheese. Add water until mixture is thicker than pancake batter but thinner than biscuit dough. Cut cheese in 1-inch squares about ½ inch thick. Dip in batter. Fry quickly on both sides in hot oil. Serve plain or with picante (see page 109).

*Possible seasoning combinations include 2 tsp. soy sauce, ¼ tsp. dry mustard (optional), and garlic; garlic, hot sauce or cayenne, and chili powder; or chili powder, cumin, and hot sauce.

CHEESE CARUMBA

A great before-dinner snack or lunch.

1 cup grated, crumbled, or diced cheese
4 Tbs. whole wheat flour
¼ to ½ tsp. salt
cayenne or hot sauce to taste
¼ tsp. cumin
1 Tbs. cold water

Combine all ingredients. Add more water or more flour if necessary to form a stiff dough. Roll thin and cut into squares. Fry on both sides in an oiled pan. Remove from pan and let sit for a few moments. Shake on more cumin, cayenne, or hot sauce as desired.

QUICHE MORAINE (serves 4 to 6)

Crust:
1¼ cups flour (white is preferred, or a mixture of wheat
    and white can be used)
½ tsp. salt
⅓ cup margarine
3 Tbs. water

Filling:
1½ cups crumbled or diced cheese
1½ cups powdered milk
1 cup powdered egg
3 cups water
2 Tbs. dried onion, rehydrated
⅛ to ¼ tsp. Tabasco or cayenne
2 Tbs. dried green and red peppers, rehydrated
salt and pepper to taste

For crust, mix flour and salt together. Cut in margarine, using two knives or spoon edges. Mix in water to form a dough. Roll out and fit into a fry pan. For filling, layer cheese on the bottom of the pie crust. Mix dry milk and egg powders in a bowl; slowly add water, stirring constantly to prevent lumping. Stir in vegetables and seasonings. Pour into crust, cover, and bake, using a twiggy fire on top, 30 minutes or until crust pulls away from side of pan and filling is set.

Hint: Fresh eggs, if available, can be used in place of the powdered eggs.

THUNDER CHILI (serves 3 to 4)

NOLS issues a vegetarian chili product containing TVP (textured vegetable protein).

4 cups water
½ cup vegetarian chili mix
2 cups potato pearls
crumbled or finely chopped cheese to taste

Boil water and add chili mix. Cook for 10 to 15 minutes. Take off heat, and mix in potato pearls until desired consistency is achieved. Add cheese to taste and stir until melted. Great alone or serve with rice or tortillas, topped with salsa or hot sauce.

LISAGNA WHIZNUT VARIATION (serves 3)

NEW!

Named for Lisa Jaeger.

½ lb. pasta (shells, spirals, or macaroni work best)
2 base packs
fresh onion slices and a couple cloves garlic, or 1 heaping
     Tbs. dried onion and 1 Tbs. garlic powder
1 can tomato paste or ½ cup dried tomato powder
spices: ½ tsp. salt, 2 heaping tsp. oregano, 2 heaping tsp.
     basil, ½ tsp. black pepper, 1 tsp. vinegar
4 rounded serving spoons flour
2 heaping tsp. baking powder
1 rounded Tbs. powdered eggs
1 rounded Tbs. powdered milk
¾ to 1 lb. of cheese

Cook pasta in salt water or with two base packs. Sauté onions and garlic in fry pan with oil or margarine. In a bowl, mix about 2 cups water and the tomato paste or powder. To this sauce, add the spices. (*Hint:* Be sure to season tomato sauce to taste before layering it over pasta. A bit of sugar can reduce the pungent tomato flavor.) In a separate container, mix flour, baking powder, eggs, and milk with approximately 2½ cups cold water. Mix to pancake batter consistency and pour over cooked, drained pasta. Stir and taste. Make sure that the pasta does not taste too bland. Layer thin slices of cheese on the bottom of the fry pan. Pour pasta mixture into fry pan over cheese slices. Spread tomato sauce over the pasta and cover with more thin slices of cheese. Sprinkle with oregano and cover. Bake over stove with twiggy fire for 20 minutes or until brown and bubbly on top. Be careful to rotate the pan over the bottom heat source so as not to burn the casserole.

  Variations: Experiment with spices, add meat, or pour the flour batter over the pasta instead of mixing it in.

SPOOZ-OLÉ (serves 3 to 4)

6 cups water
2 to 4 Tbs. dried green and red peppers
1 to 2 base packs
2 to 3 cups pasta (other than spaghetti)
2 cups instant refried or black beans
1 Tbs. dried onion
1½ tsp. black pepper
1 Tbs. garlic
1 Tbs. oregano
1 Tbs. chili powder
⅓ to ½ lb. cheddar or jack cheese

Add peppers and base packs to water and bring to a boil. Add pasta and cook until tender. In a separate container, rehydrate the beans, onion, and spices with some of the boiling pasta water until a gravylike consistency is achieved. Season to taste. Drain the pasta and stir into the beans. Add grated or chunked cheese, stir, and let melt. Depending on the consistency you end up with, you can either dip tortillas into it like a stew or fill tortillas with the mixture and roll up and eat. Enjoy!

 ## PEGGY'S TAMALE PIE (serves 3)

Pie crust:
2½ cups cornmeal
2 tsp. baking powder
1 tsp. salt
1 Tbs. oil
1 cup water

Mix ingredients until moistened; dough will resemble biscuit dough. Flatten into pan and cook until dryish on top, using round the clock rotation method. Be careful not to burn the bottom. When crust is done, spread a little margarine over the surface and poke a few holes in the hot crust to drench and moisten.

Filling mix:
4 cups boiled water (approximate)
2 cups instant refried or black beans
¼ cup tomato base
2 tsp. garlic
1 tsp. pepper
1 tsp. cumin
cayenne and hot sauce to taste
½ lb. sliced cheese

Add all filling ingredients (except cheese) to boiled water, stir until mixed, and take off heat. Place half of cheese on crust, then spread filling mixture over the top of the cheese and add the remainder of the cheese. Cover and bake with a twiggy fire until cheese on top is brown and bubbly. If pie starts to burn, a small amount of water on the side of the pan will steam and melt the cheese.

Variation: Instead of black beans, use lentils or lentils and rice and delete the tomato base.

VEGETARIAN MEATBALLS
(makes 22 to 25 meatballs)

These can be eaten cold as a trail food, added to casseroles, or served with egg noodles and gravy (see page 108) or with spaghetti.

¾ cup cornmeal
½ cup whole wheat flour
¼ cup white flour
6 Tbs. dry milk powder
½ tsp. garlic
½ tsp. salt
1 Tbs. dried onion
1 tsp. soy sauce
1 Tbs. oil
½ to ¾ cup water

Mix all dry ingredients together. Add rehydrated onions, mixing well to make a stiff dough. Form 22 to 25 balls, approximately the size of a walnut. Add about 1 Tbs. oil to a fry pan and heat. Add grain balls and shake around until they are coated with oil. Cover and cook 20 to 30 minutes, shaking occasionally to be sure they brown on all sides. Eat warm or cold.

Tip: Plan ahead with a few gourmet extras. These treats can be a culinary highlight on long trip: Pesto sauce, sun dried tomatoes, fresh garlic, olive oil, dried shitake or morrel mushrooms. Check with a specialty food store for these as well as tubes of concentrated garlic and tomato pastes, perfect for that special camp menu!

MEXICAN GRITS AND CHEESE CASSEROLE (serves 4 to 6)

5 cups water
1½ cups grits
2 tsp. salt
5 Tbs. powdered egg
½ cup water
2 tsp. chili powder
1 tsp. cumin (optional)
hot sauce to taste
4 to 6 Tbs. margarine or bacon grease
1½ cups cheese, grated or diced small

Bring 5 cups water to a boil. Stir in grits and salt. Cook, stirring, until thickened. Mix egg with ½ cup water. Add to grits with spices, hot sauce, margarine, and most of cheese. Pour into a greased frying pan. Cover with remaining cheese. Bake, covered, over low heat 30 to 45 minutes. Serve garnished with Grapenuts for crunch and more hot sauce.

Hint: Grits need to sit covered for 15 minutes to solidify.

Soups

Soups are a good source of protein, fats, and carbohydrates and can be a great way to use up leftover ingredients. They make a quick warm-up meal with a hearty bread accompaniment.

DUMPLINGS (serves 3 to 4)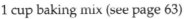

A recipe from the original NOLS Cookery.

1 cup baking mix (see page 63)
½ cup cornmeal
½ cup water
1 tsp. salt

Mix all ingredients, spoon into small 1-inch balls, and place in boiling soup or stew. Cover and steam cook for 5 to 10 minutes. Dumplings are a good way to make a soup or stew heartier and more filling. Try making cup-of-soup in a pot with dumplings and cheese for a quick, high-calorie meal.

BASIC BROTH SOUP (serves 4 to 6)

6 to 8 cups water
1 to 3 Tbs. or 1 to 3 packets base of choice, or use bouillon cubes or packets
1 to 1½ cups solid ingredients (assorted pastas, grains, dried and fresh vegetables)
salt to taste
spices to taste
3 to 4 Tbs. margarine

Boil water; add bases to taste. Add solid ingredients. Vegetables and rice take 20 to 30 minutes to cook, so add these first. Noodles take 10 to 15 minutes. Add spices while solids are cooking. When solids are done, stir in margarine and salt (if necessary).

Note: If using tomato base, add it after solid ingredients are cooked.

Variation: To make basic cream soup, thicken with potato pearls or 2 to 3 Tbs. flour mixed into 4 Tbs. water and added to the soup; or mix ½ to 1 cup powdered milk into ½ cup water and stir into soup; heat through and serve.

MINESTRONE SOUP (serves 3)

3½ to 4½ cups water
¾ cup dried refried beans
3 Tbs. dried vegetable soup mix (cup-of-soup mix will do)
3 Tbs. dried peas and carrots
2 Tbs. dried peppers
2 Tbs. dried onion
2 to 3 base packets (chicken or vegetable works well)
1 tsp. black pepper
1 tsp. garlic
1 tsp. basil
2 tsp. soy sauce
½ lb. pasta (two types, if possible)

Bring 3½ to 4 cups water to a boil and add all ingredients except pasta. Set aside, covered. Cook pasta and drain. Bring soup back to a boil, and check that ingredients are hydrated. If soup has become too thick, thin by adding some of the pasta water. Add pasta and bring to temperature.

Variations: Use leftover pasta in soup or bulk up soup by adding cubed cheese, pepperoni, crackers, or croutons. For a heartier version, make dumplings on top.

POTATO CHEESE SOUP (serves 2 to 3)

½ cup potato pearls
1 cup crumbled cheddar
½ cup powdered milk
2 Tbs. flour
2 Tbs. dried onion
4 cups water
½ tsp. salt
½ tsp. pepper
1 tsp. oil

Put all ingredients except potatoes and cheese into a pot. Bring to a boil, stirring often. Put potato pearls in a bowl and add enough of the hot soup to form a thin paste. Pour this back into the soup; stir. Add cheese and cook, stirring until melted. Serve hot with bread. Good with a dash of cayenne, hot sauce, or dry mustard powder.

Variation: Add chopped bacon or ham

Hint: Dumplings (see page 105) are great additions to all kinds of soups and make a mug of soup into a meal.

MISO SOUP WITH VEGETABLES (serves 3)

Great for digestive problems. Note: Do not add boiling water to miso, as it will make the nutrient enzymes in the miso ineffective.

1 Tbs. dried onion or 1 medium onion, diced
2 Tbs. dried peas and carrots or 2 carrots, diced
2 Tbs. margarine
4½ cups water
1 to 2 Tbs. miso

Rehydrate onions, peas, and carrots for about 5 minutes. Melt margarine in pot. Add vegetables and sauté about 2 to 3 minutes. Add water and heat to boiling. If using fresh vegetables, boil until tender, then remove from heat. Put miso in a bowl; add some of the soup (cooled a little) and blend. Pour miso back into soup and stir.

Variation: Pour boiling water into a mug and, after letting it cool slightly, stir in miso to taste. Serve.

Sauces

Your imagination in sauce making can often spell the difference between a so-so meal and a great one. A basic white sauce takes on many different personalities with the addition of spices, bases, dried vegetables, and cheese.

BASIC WHITE SAUCE (makes about 1 cup)

> 3 Tbs. margarine or bacon grease
> 3 Tbs. flour (white makes a lighter sauce)
> 1 cup water or milk
> salt and pepper to taste (omit salt if you plan to add a
>   base)

Melt margarine in a saucepan. Stir in flour and let it cook for a few minutes, being careful not to burn it. Add water or milk slowly, stirring to mix. Season with salt and pepper and cook, stirring constantly so sauce doesn't stick and burn, until thickened and heated through.

Variations: To the completed white sauce, add one of the following:

- 2 Tbs. tomato base, garlic, ¼ tsp. oregano and/or basil for an Italian sauce.
- ½ Tbs. chicken or beef base for a gravy that is good with mixed vegetables and noodles.
- 2 Tbs. cheese base, ¼ tsp. dry mustard powder, dash black pepper.
- 1 to 2 tsp. curry powder for an Indian-style sauce with rice and raisins.
- 1 cup grated or cubed cheese.
- 1 to 2 packets cup-of-soup mix.

Note: Taste the sauce after adding a base. It may be salty enough. The longer the sauce cooks, the thicker it gets, so you may need to add more liquid, especially in these variety sauces. Adding water can help smooth out the consistency and dilute excess salt flavor.

Hint: The best cheese sauces and macaroni dishes have a white sauce base.

KETCHUP (makes ½ cup)

¼ cup tomato base
3 Tbs. brown sugar
1 Tbs. mustard
1 tsp. black pepper
1 tsp. garlic
pinch of salt
3 Tbs. vinegar
1 Tbs. soy sauce
water

Mix all dry ingredients together thoroughly. Stir in vinegar, soy sauce, and water until desired consistency is achieved.

NOLS PICANTE SAUCE (makes about 1 cup)

The test panel gave this a rave review.

1 Tbs. dried onion
1 Tbs. dried green and red peppers
1 cup water (½ hot and ½ cold)
2 Tbs. tomato base
dash garlic powder
¼ tsp. hot sauce or cayenne (to taste)
1 tsp. each vinegar and brown sugar (optional, but adds good flavor)
dash black pepper

Rehydrate onions and peppers in ½ cup hot water. Add tomato base and stir until well mixed. Add remaining ingredients and ½ cup cold water. Mix well. You can thin this out more if you wish. Serve cold over nachos, main dishes, potato-cheese patties, or bean and lentil dishes.

SPICY PEANUT SAUCE

Great change of pace for noodles or rice. See Gado-gado Spaghetti recipe under Pastas for sauce procedure.

Variation: Stir 1 Tbs. miso into sauce for peanut-miso flavor.

SPAGHETTI SAUCE (makes about 1½ cups)

    1 Tbs. dried onion
    1 Tbs. dried green and red peppers
    1½ cups water (approximate)
    4 to 6 Tbs. tomato base
    2 Tbs. powdered milk (optional)
    ½ tsp. oregano and/or basil
    ¼ tsp. black pepper
    ¼ to ½ tsp. garlic

Rehydrate onion and peppers in ½ cup hot water for 5 to 10 minutes. Stir in remaining ingredients, except last 1 cup water. Gradually add water. Heat through, stirring occasionally, and serve over cooked pasta. This can be thinned with more water if you wish.

MEXICAN SAUCE (makes about 1 cup)

1 Tbs. dried onion
1 Tbs. dried green and red peppers
1¼ cups hot water
3 Tbs. tomato base
½ tsp. chili powder
cumin to taste
dash cayenne or hot sauce

Rehydrate onions and peppers in ¼ cup hot water for 5 to 10 minutes. Add remaining water and ingredients and heat through, stirring occasionally. Serve with beans and tortillas or give a Mexican flavor to rice or pastas. Our taste testers loved it on pizza.

BREADSTUFFS

Quick Breads

BASIC QUICK BREAD

⅔ cup whole wheat flour
⅔ cup white flour
⅓ cup powdered milk
1½ tsp. baking powder
½ tsp. salt
2 heaping Tbs. margarine
1½ cups water

Mix all ingredients. Pour into a fry pan, cover, and bake over a twiggy fire about 15 minutes or until done.

Variations:

- Fruit and nut quick bread: Make basic recipe and add 2 Tbs. brown sugar and ½ cup chopped fruits and/or nuts of your choice. Bake as above.
- Italian quick bread: To the basic quick bread recipe add 1 tsp. garlic powder, 1 tsp. crushed oregano, 1 tsp. dill (optional), 2 tsp. vinegar (optional), 3 Tbs. Parmesan, and 1 Tbs. dried onion (rehydrated in hot water, then drained). Mix all ingredients together and bake as above.

Hint: You can use any combination of white and wheat flours in most bread recipes. More wheat flour will produce a heavier, denser bread; more white flour, a lighter, fluffier bread.

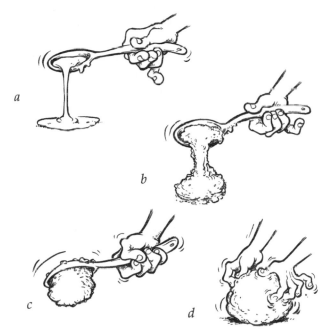

Different consistencies of batter/dough: a. pancake batter: very thin and runny: will spead quicky to form thin pancakes. b. muffin batter: thicker and lumpier: will still pour but just barely. c. biscuit dough: doughy, too sticky to fall off the spoon. d. bread dough: thicken further until dough forms a ball

CORNBREAD

1 cup cornmeal
½ cup whole wheat flour
⅓ cup white flour
⅔ cup powdered milk
1 Tbs. baking powder
1 tsp. salt
1½ cups water
½ tsp. vanilla
3 Tbs. honey or brown sugar

Mix together dry ingredients. Gradually add water, vanilla, and sweetener, stirring well. Pour into a greased fry pan, cover, and bake using a twiggy fire for about 15 minutes or until done (when a pine needle or thin stick poked into the middle comes out clean, or the bread springs back when touched in the center).

Variation: For Mexican cornbread, make the following changes: reduce honey or sugar to 1½ Tbs. and add 1 cup jack cheese (crumbled or diced small), ⅛ tsp. hot sauce, 1 tsp. cumin, ¼ tsp. cayenne, and 2 to 3 Tbs. dried peppers (rehydrated in hot water, then drained). Bake as above.

FRUIT BREAD

⅔ cup white flour
⅓ cup whole wheat flour
⅓ cup powdered milk
3 Tbs. brown sugar
1 Tbs. powdered egg
1½ tsp. baking powder
½ tsp. salt
¼ tsp. cinnamon or nutmeg
1 cup dried fruit, chopped (banana chips are great, if
    available)
⅔ cup chopped nuts
¼ cup margarine, melted
¾ to 1¼ cups water

Combine all dry ingredients, including fruit and nuts; mix. Stir in melted margarine and add water gradually to form a pancake-type batter. Pour into fry pan, cover, and bake using a twiggy fire for 15 to 25 minutes or until done.

PEANUT BUTTER BREAD

½ cup peanut butter
½ cup honey
2 heaping Tbs. margarine, melted
1 cup whole wheat flour
1 cup white flour
¾ cup powdered milk
2 Tbs. powdered egg
½ tsp. salt
1½ tsp. baking powder
1 cup dried fruit, chopped
2 cups water

Mix peanut butter, honey, and margarine. Blend dry ingredients, including fruit. Add dry mix and water to peanut butter mixture and stir well. Bake in covered fry pan approximately 25 minutes, using a twiggy fire.

Variations: Add ½ cup of one or more of the following: chopped nuts, coconut, or chocolate or other flavored chips.

Yeast Breads

Yeast consists of tiny one-cell organisms that are dormant until combined with warm water and sugar or starch. Water that is too hot kills the yeast; water that is too cold will not activate it. As the yeast grows and multiplies, carbon dioxide gas is given off causing the dough to rise.

Flour, salt, water, and yeast constitute the basics of bread, to which other ingredients are added for variety. Wheat flour is best because it is high in gluten, fibers that become elastic when kneaded and hold the gas pockets created by the yeast. Other flours (graham, buckwheat, and so forth) are tasty but require more skill in handling. We recommend making basic breads that usually work well even under less than ideal conditions.

Hint: 110°F is the standard water temperature used to activate yeast. When a warm clean finger is placed in the water, it should feel quite warm but not hot to the touch. If it is difficult to keep your finger in the water for more than 5 seconds, the water is too hot and should be left to cool for a few minutes.

BASIC BREAD

1 level Tbs. yeast
1½ cups lukewarm water (drop a few drops by spoon onto your wrist to test the temperature)
2 Tbs. sugar
2 tsp. salt
2 Tbs. margarine or oil (optional)
3 to 3½ cups flour (⅓ whole wheat, ⅔ white is good)

Dissolve yeast in lukewarm water with sugar, and salt. Cover and let sit for about 5 minutes in warm spot until it froths. (Try putting it in an insulated mug and capping it. When frothed, it bubbles through the hole a little.) Add half the flour and beat vigorously 2 to 3 minutes to develop gluten; the wet batter will smooth out and start to get a little stringy. Add margarine and remaining flour to get a thick dough. Flour your hands and knead the bread on a floured fry pan. Knead with the heels of your clean hands for about 8 minutes, folding when dough becomes too sticky to handle. The dough will be silky and springy when done. Shape into a loaf and place in a well-oiled pot or fry pan. Press dough out to touch the edges, and grease the top of the loaf with oil or margarine. Cover and set in a warm place to rise for about 1 hour, or until doubled in size. If it's a very cold day, let the dough rise by placing it on top of a pan of boiling water with a cover over it. Once risen, bake the bread 30 to 50 minutes using a twiggy fire or the flip baking method. When done, the bread will be golden brown and will have a hollow sound when thumped. Take it out of the pan and cool in a spot with good air circulation 5 to 10 minutes before cutting.

Variations: Pinch off pieces of dough and bake as large rolls rather than a loaf, or try the following:

- Onion-cheese bread: Add 1 Tbs. base instead of salt, 1 to 2 Tbs. rehydrated onion (using onion water as part of the recipe water), and 1 cup crumbled or diced cheese (optional, but if not using cheese, increase onion to 3 Tbs.).
- Cinnamon-raisin yeast bread: Add ½ cup raisins, 2 tsp. cinnamon, and ½ cup sugar to the yeast water, and follow basic recipe.
- Nut-fruit yeast bread: Add 1 cup chopped fruit, nuts, and seeds to the basic recipe.
- Oatmeal or cereal yeast bread: Replace 1 cup of wheat flour with 1 cup of oatmeal or other cereal.

Hint: To use the dough the next morning, put it in a plastic bag, squeeze out the air, tie a knot in the bag, and put it into another bag left untied. Sleep with the dough overnight to keep it warm. (Don't do this in bear country!)

DINNER BREAD

1 cup warm water
2 Tbs. yeast
1 Tbs. brown sugar or honey
3 Tbs. margarine or oil
3 cups flour (half whole wheat and half white, or use all of
    one type)
2 Tbs. powdered milk
2 Tbs. powdered egg
½ Tbs. salt
1 cup cooked grains, beans, or potatoes

In a bowl, add water, yeast, sugar, and margarine. Set aside for 5 minutes to activate yeast. In another bowl, mix together half the flour with the other dry ingredients. Add in the grains and stir, then add in the yeast mixture, stirring well. Work the remaining flour in as you're kneading the dough. It should have a smooth, elastic consistency. Knead 5 minutes. Cover the dough with a pot lid and let sit in the sun or in a warm place for 45 minutes to double in size, then punch down and form a loaf. Let rise again for about 20 minutes in a greased pan, or you can let it rise only once in a greased pan. (Letting dough rise twice makes a lighter bread.) Bake on stove over low heat, using a twiggy fire, for 20 to 35 minutes or until done. It should have a moist, chewy consistency.

Variation: Experiment with spices or other flavorings.

FRY BREAD (serves 2)

2 tsp. yeast
1 tsp. salt
¾ cup warm water
1 tsp. sugar
1¾ to 2 cups flour (a mix of white and whole wheat is
    good)
oil for frying

Mix all ingredients except flour and oil. Let stand 5 minutes. Add flour and knead until smooth. Let rise. Heat oil in fry pan. Flatten dough into a fat tortilla ½ inch thick. Fry bread on both sides. Serve with a spread of honey or brown sugar, margarine, and cinnamon. How much oil you use for frying determines the crust and texture of this bread. Real fry bread uses a lot of oil, but it is not necessary. You can cut down on fat calories by just oiling the pan. If you double this recipe, cook half at a time.

Variation: For Indian fry bread, mix bread as above and use immediately without allowing it to rise.

Biscuits

BASIC BISCUITS (makes 10 to 12)

2 cups baking mix (see page 63)
4 Tbs. margarine
½ to ¾ cup water

Cut margarine into baking mix using spoon edges. Add enough water to form a stiff dough. Knead in bowl about a dozen times. Pinch off enough dough for desired size biscuit; pat into shape. Bake in covered fry pan, using a twiggy fire, for about 15 to 20 minutes or until done. As an alternative to baking, fry in melted margarine until both sides are browned. Cover and cook on low heat about 8 to 10 minutes. Good served with margarine and a white sauce.

Variations: For cheesy biscuits, Add ½ tsp. garlic powder and some rehydrated onions to dough. Form into balls and pull apart into halves. Insert a piece of cheese and pinch halves back together. Bake as above. For fruit and nut biscuits, mix together 1 Tbs. margarine, 1 Tbs. brown sugar, and ⅓ cup chopped mixed fruits and nuts, and insert into biscuits using the method just described.

CHICKEN BISCUITS

1½ cups flour
¼ cup cornmeal
1 tsp. baking powder
1 to 2 tsp. chicken base (or any other base)
2 Tbs. margarine
1 to 2 tsp. dried onion rehydrated in ½ cup water or milk

Mix dry ingredients except cornmeal; cut in margarine. Stir in water (with onions) to form a dough. Pinch off pieces and make thin cakes. Roll cakes in cornmeal. Oil and heat a fry pan. Bake, covered, for about 20 minutes using a twiggy fire.

Muffins

WHOLE WHEAT–CORNMEAL CHEESE MUFFINS

1 cup whole wheat flour
½ cup cornmeal
¼ cup cheese powder (optional)
1 heaping Tbs. powdered milk
1 heaping Tbs. powdered egg
1½ tsp. baking powder
¾ to 1 cup water
½ cup crumbled or cubed cheese

Mix all dry ingredients. Add water gradually, stirring to form a slightly sticky dough. Mix in the cheese. Spoon mixture onto hot oiled pan. Cover and cook over medium heat until top is fairly set, then flip and finish cooking. Takes about 20 to 25 minutes. Good trail food.

Variation: For sweet muffins, omit cheese and add raisins and nuts or chocolate chips (about ½ cup total), vanilla, cinnamon, and 1 Tbs. brown sugar. Serve with honey, peanut butter, or margarine.

OAT SCONES (makes 6 to 8 large scones)

Oatmeal scones are great plain or with honey, peanut butter, wild berry jam (see page 128), or cheese. They are also excellent with soups or casseroles and make a good trail food.

½ cup margarine
2 cups oatmeal
1½ tsp. baking powder
pinch of salt (allows recipe to use less sweetener)
¼ cup honey or brown sugar
½ tsp. vanilla (omit for a less sweet taste)
water
2 cups white flour

Melt margarine in a pot and stir in oatmeal to soak it up. Add baking powder, salt, honey, and vanilla; mix thoroughly. Add water and flour alternately until mixture is neither too sticky nor too dry to hold together well. Form 4-inch patties about ¾ inch thick. These can be cooked by frying on both sides until done, but they come out much lighter, with better flavor, when baked with a twiggy fire for about 20 to 25 minutes or until cooked through.

Variation: Boil dried fruit in water until mushy. Add sugar to taste and some flour to soak up water and use as a filling. Place a spoonful between two thin patties, seal edges, and bake. Makes a giant Fig Newton–type pastry.

CROWNS À LA SIERRA (makes 8 to 10)

This recipe was an instant hit!

2 cups baking mix (see page 63)
½ cup brown sugar
1 tsp. nutmeg or cinnamon
3 heaping Tbs. margarine
½ to ¾ cup water
filling (see below)

Mix dry ingredients. Cut in margarine. Add water to make a stiff dough. Pinch off dough and roll into balls. Bake in fry pan, using a twiggy fire, for 5 minutes, then indent middle with a spoon and continue baking until brown, about 15 to 20 minutes more. Just before serving, fill depression in center with filling.

Filling:
½ cup nuts and chopped fruit (a good combination is
    raisins, chopped walnuts, and chopped apricots)
3 Tbs. honey or brown sugar (with sugar, add 1 Tbs.
    water)
1 heaping Tbs. margarine
dash of salt
½ tsp. cinnamon or nutmeg

Mix together and cook over low heat a few minutes until
smooth.

Specialties

CORN TORTILLAS (makes 12)

2 cups cornmeal
½ cup whole wheat flour
½ tsp. salt
⅔ to 1 cup water

Mix dry ingredients. Add water until you get a smooth dough
that easily forms a ball. It should not be sticky or too dry to
hold its shape. Knead for about 5 minutes. Cover and let sit 15
minutes. Divide into 12 balls. Place one ball at a time in the
middle of a plastic bag and roll into a 5- to 6-inch circle. Cook
quickly on both sides in a hot, unoiled fry pan until golden
brown.

FLOUR TORTILLAS (makes 12)

3 cups white flour
¼ tsp. salt
1 tsp. baking powder (optional—makes a puffier tortilla)
¼ cup margarine
½ cup warm water

Mix dry ingredients together. Cut in margarine, using two knives or spoon edges. Add water and mix well with your hands. Proceed as for corn tortillas above.

Uses for tortillas:

- Melt cheese on top for quesadillas; serve with picante or hot sauce.
- Add margarine, hot sauce, and cheese to warmed-up leftover grains such as rice or couscous and roll up in a tortilla.
- Quickly fry a flour tortilla in hot oil in a fry pan (it will puff up) and serve with stewed apples or other fruit or sprinkle with cinnamon and sugar.
- Cover tortillas with spicy cooked beans and cheese, roll up, and place in a fry pan. Cover with Mexican sauce and cook (covered) until heated through.
- Use as a bread for any sandwich.
- Spread with power peanut butter (see page 128) and raisins and roll up.
- Break cooked tortillas into large pieces, fry in hot oil, melt cheese on top, and serve with picante (see page 109) for nachos.

CHAPPATIES (makes 4 5-inch flat breads)

½ cup flour (whole wheat is more authentic, but white is okay too)
½ cup cornmeal
pinch of salt
½ cup water
margarine for frying
toppings: sliced cheese, bacon bits, chopped wild onions, cayenne or Tabasco

Mix all ingredients except margarine and toppings. Form in very thin patties and fry in lightly greased pan until golden brown. After they are turned, add desired toppings; cover pan to help cheese melt.

Variations: Combine 1 cup whole wheat flour, ¼ tsp. salt, 1 Tbs. margarine, ¼ cup water. Proceed as for making chappaties.

EMPANADAS (makes 10 to 12 Mexican Turnovers)

2 cups flour
2 tsp. baking powder
1 tsp. salt (use only ¼ tsp. if you fry in margarine rather than oil)
½ cup margarine
⅓ to ½ cup reconstituted milk
filling (see below)
margarine or oil for frying

Mix flour, baking powder, and salt. Cut in ½ cup margarine. Add milk to form a pie crust dough. Roll out thin and cut into 4-inch circles. On half of each circle, place a small spoonful of filling. Fold the other half over and use a little powdered egg mixed with water to seal turnovers. Heat margarine or oil in fry pan. Fry empanadas on both sides until dough is cooked.

Fillings:
- Mixture of brown sugar and margarine.
- To mixture of chopped dried fruit (let sit in hot water a while, then drain), add 1 Tbs. margarine, 2 Tbs. chopped nuts, and 1 Tbs. flour if it seems too juicy.
- Mixture of canned chicken, chopped cheese, and curry powder.

YEAST CINNAMON ROLLS

An impressive specialty at home or on the trail.

1 basic bread dough recipe
4 Tbs. margarine
½ to 1 cup brown sugar
1 Tbs. cinnamon
½ cup nuts (optional)
½ cup raisins (optional)

Mix up basic bread recipe and roll out into a large rectangle
½ inch thick. Mix margarine, brown sugar, and cinnamon
until creamy and spread it on the dough. Sprinkle with nuts

Steps To Great Cinnamon Rolls

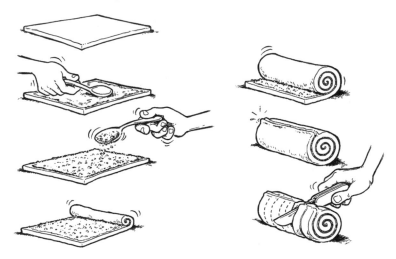

*Roll dough into a large rectangle, ½ inch thick. Spread the surface of
the dough with margarine. sugar and cinnamon mixture. Start from
one long side and roll the dough. When roll is complete, taper the
end of the dough and pinch shut to seal in the sugar. Cut roll into
slices 1 inch thick.*

and raisins if desired. Roll up jelly-roll style, pinching dough closed so sugar doesn't fall out. Slice roll into 1-inch slices and place in pan. Cover and bake, using a twiggy fire, for 25 to 35 minutes or until done. (You can pinch the undersides of rolls together before putting them into the pan to prevent hot sugar from leaking out and scorching, but with good baking techniques, that leakage can form a delicious glaze.)

Variation: Substitute apple cider mix for sugar and cinnamon.

Hint: Dental floss makes a great tool for cutting the cinnamon roll log. Use it like a cheese wire.

QUICK CINNAMON ROLLS

3 cups baking mix (see page 63)
1 to 1½ cups water
¾ Tbs. cinnamon
¼ cup raisins
¼ cup nuts
3 Tbs. margarine
½ cup brown sugar
extra flour for rolling

Mix together baking mix and water. Roll out on floured surface, adding more flour to make dough less sticky if necessary. Follow procedure for yeast cinnamon rolls, above. Bake for 15 to 25 minutes.

Spreadables

All the following are good in hot cereal and on crackers, bagels, biscuits, pancakes, bread, and muffins.

POWER PEANUT BUTTER SPREAD
(makes about 1 cup)

½ cup peanut butter
¼ cup honey
¼ cup margarine
⅓ cup powdered milk

Carefully melt peanut butter, honey, and margarine in a pot. Stir in powdered milk.

Variations: Add sunflower seeds, chopped nuts, raisins, chopped dried fruit.

WILD BERRY JAM

2 cups fresh berries
½ to 1 cup brown sugar
1 to 2 Tbs. flour to thicken if desired

Wash berries and crush them. Measure out 2 cups and put into pan. Bring to a boil. Add sugar and flour. Cook rapidly until thick. Stir frequently to prevent burning.

CINNAMON-HONEY "BUTTER"

Mix ¼ cup margarine with 1 Tbs. honey and ¼ tsp. cinnamon.

DESSERTS AND SNACKS

BASIC CAKE RECIPE (for a 12-inch fry pan)

1½ cups baking mix (see page 63)
½ cup flour
½ cup powdered milk
2 level Tbs. powdered egg
pinch salt
4 Tbs. brown sugar or honey
1½ cups cold water (approximate—for a pourable batter)
2 to 3 Tbs. margarine, melted
1 tsp. vanilla

Mix all dry ingredients. Add liquid ingredients and mix until lumps are gone. Pour into greased, floured fry pan. Cover and bake, using a twiggy fire, 15 to 25 minutes or until done (see hint on page 130). Loosen and remove from pan. Cool and frost, or try variations.

Variations:
- Chocolate: Use ¾ cup cocoa mix instead of powdered milk.
- Cinnamon-raisin: Add ½ cup softened, drained raisins and 1 tsp. cinnamon or nutmeg.
- Peanut: Omit salt, add ½ cup crushed peanuts and ½ cup extra sugar.
- Lemon Jell-O: Make plain cake, remove from pan, poke holes in top with fork or very small twig; dissolve 3 Tbs. lemon (or other flavor) Jell-O in ½ cup boiling water. Spoon over top of cake and let sit 10 minutes before serving.

- Pudding: Make plain cake, remove from pan, cool 10 minutes. Cut cake in half horizontally. Mix up a thick pudding with instant pudding mix using less milk, and fill between layers. Frost with butterscotch or chocolate frosting (see pages 136–137).

Hint: A cake is done if it springs back when touched lightly in the middle, or when a pine needle inserted into the center comes out clean.

LUCY SMITH'S FRUIT CAKE
(for a 12-inch fry pan)

1 cup dried fruit, chopped
½ cup raisins (optional)
1 tsp. cinnamon or nutmeg
1¼ to 1½ cups water
2 cups baking mix (see page 63)
½ cup powdered milk
¼ cup apple cider mix or 4 Tbs. brown sugar or honey
2 Tbs. powdered egg
pinch of salt
1 tsp. vanilla
2 to 3 Tbs. melted margarine

Put fruit, raisins, and cinnamon or nutmeg in pan with water to cover. Bring to boil; simmer 10 minutes. Cool. Mix all other dry ingredients. Drain water off fruit. Add this water, vanilla, and margarine to dry ingredients. Stir well. Mix in drained fruit. Pour into greased and floured 12-inch fry pan. Cover and bake about 25 minutes or until done (see hint above), using a twiggy fire. If you are using a topping such as chopped nuts, additional fruit, or chocolate chips, sprinkle it on the cake halfway through baking time.

FRUITY UPSIDE DOWN CAKE

Make up basic cake batter (see page 129). Melt 2 Tbs. margarine in 12-inch fry pan. Mix in 3 to 4 Tbs. brown sugar and spread over bottom of pan. Place dried fruit (pineapple is best) on sugar mixture. Pour batter over fruit. Bake, using a twiggy fire, for 15 to 25 minutes.

COFFEE CAKE (for a 12-inch fry pan)

1¾ cup flour
½ cup brown sugar
⅓ cup powdered milk
1 Tbs. powdered egg
2 tsp. baking powder
½ tsp. salt
4 Tbs. margarine, melted
1 tsp. vanilla
½ cup water

Grease and flour pan. In a separate container, mix dry ingredients; add liquids and stir. Pour mixture into pan and bake 12 to 18 minutes, using a twiggy fire. Serve with stewed spiced apples or wild berry sauce poured over each serving. Also good plain or with honey-cinnamon butter.
Variations:
- Streusel coffee cake: Sprinkle with a topping made from 5 Tbs. brown sugar, ⅓ cup oatmeal, 4 Tbs. margarine, and 1 tsp. cinnamon mixed together. Bake, using a twiggy fire, for 15 to 25 minutes.
- Blueberry coffee cake: Cook 1 cup fresh berries or drained canned fruit with 1 Tbs. sugar or honey, 2 Tbs. margarine, 2 Tbs. flour, and about ¾ cup water. It should be quite thick. Spread over basic coffee cake batter and bake as above.

- Gingerbread coffee cake: Make basic recipe, except use 1 cup flour and 1 cup gingerbread mix; reduce sugar to ¼ to ⅓ cup, reduce baking powder to 1 tsp., reduce salt to ¼ tsp. Bake as above.

CHEESECAKE

Crust:
3 Tbs. margarine
1 Tbs. brown sugar
1½ cups Grapenuts or granola
3 to 4 Tbs. water

Melt margarine and sugar in fry pan. Add Grapenuts and stir for 2 to 3 minutes. Add water and stir another minute. Remove from heat. Use back of spoon to press Grapenuts evenly over bottom and 1 inch up sides of pan. Set aside to cool.

Filling:
2 cups cheesecake mix (¾ lb.)
6 Tbs. powdered milk
1 tsp. vanilla (optional)
2 to 2½ cups water

Add water slowly to other ingredients, blending to avoid lumps. Pour into cooled crust. Put in cool place to set.
Variations:

- Drain some liquid from canned blueberries or other fruit and mix 1 to 1½ Tbs. flour into it. Pour fruit and remaining juice into pot. Heat; stir in flour mixture. Cook until thick, stirring frequently. Cool. Pour over set cheesecake. Or drain liquid from berries and just spoon some berries over each serving. If fresh berries are available, make topping used for blueberry coffee cake (above).

- Chocolate cheesecake: Proceed as above, but add ⅓ cup cocoa mix to filling. Add chocolate or carob chips if desired.
- Substitute instant pudding for cheesecake mix and make according to basic recipe.

Hint: Cakes can be mixed and cooked right in the same pan. Just grease the pan well, then add the ingredients according to the recipe, mix in the pan, and bake.

SCRAMBLED BROWNIES OR GINGERBREAD

2 cups brownie mix or gingerbread mix
6 Tbs. water (more if batter is dry)

Mix together. Spread in oiled fry pan. Cover and cook on low heat about 15 minutes until product is done on top. Scrape out of pan with a spatula. Let sit a few minutes before eating so it can stiffen. This is an alternative to baking with a twiggy fire. The end product is chewy and gooey.

Variations: Add chopped nuts, dried fruits, or chocolate chips to the mix before cooking.

DRIED FRUIT CRISP

1½ cups dried fruit, chopped
½ cup raisins
½ tsp. cinnamon or nutmeg
¼ tsp. salt
hot water to just cover fruit
½ cup chopped nuts

Combine all ingredients except nuts in a pot and let soak until fruit rehydrates—about 15 minutes. Meanwhile, combine the following:

¼ to ½ cup oatmeal
3 Tbs. flour
3 Tbs. brown sugar
4 heaping Tbs. margarine
pinch salt

Mix together to a crumbly consistency. Grease a fry pan. Add nuts to fruit mixture and pour into pan. (If there is a lot of liquid, stir in 1 Tbs. flour.) Cover with oatmeal mix. Bake, using a twiggy fire, for about 15 minutes until heated through and browned on top.

FRUIT STRUDEL

2 cups flour
¼ tsp. salt
1 tsp. baking powder
¾ cup milk (5 Tbs. powdered milk and water to make
    ¾ cup)
2 Tbs. melted margarine

Mix dry ingredients. Add milk and margarine to make a dough. Roll out to a rectangle.

Filling:
2 cups dried fruit
½ cup chopped nuts
½ cup brown sugar or ⅓ cup honey
1 tsp. cinnamon or apple pie spice mix
water to cover
1 to 2 Tbs. flour

Combine all ingredients, except flour, in a pan and bring to a boil. Add flour to 2 Tbs. of hot liquid, mix, and return to pot. Cook gently until fruit is tender. Cool. Brush dough with margarine. Spread on filling; roll up, seal ends, and bake, using

a twiggy fire, about 15 to 25 minutes or until crust is done.
(You can also brush the top of the dough with margarine
before baking.)

FRUIT COBBLER

1½ cups water
1 to 1½ cups dried fruit (mixed fruit works well)
¼ cup chopped walnuts
2 Tbs. brown sugar
1 heaping Tbs. margarine
1 tsp. cinnamon
pinch salt
1 cup baking mix cut with 1 Tbs. margarine
½ cup flour
¼ cup powdered milk
¾ cup water

Put 1 cup water, fruit, nuts, salt, margarine, brown sugar, and
cinnamon into a pan and bring to a boil. Cook for several
minutes to rehydrate, then add another ½ cup water. Mix
remaining ingredients together to form a stiff dough. Drop by
spoonfuls onto gently boiling fruit. Cover and steam about
10 minutes until pastry dumplings are done.

Variation: For Southern Cobbler, combine flour, powdered
milk, and baking mix, and add water to achieve a thick batter.
Melt 3 Tbs. margarine in fry pan, and pour in dough mixture.
Add hydrated fruit and nuts to the top; sprinkle with brown
sugar, cinnamon, and granola. Bake with a twiggy fire for
approximately 20 minutes.

PEANUT BUTTER FUDGE

½ lb. brownie mix
4 to 5 Tbs. peanut butter
2½ Tbs. sugar
2½ Tbs. powdered milk
2½ tsp. vanilla
water

Mix first four ingredients together. Add vanilla, and slowly add drops of water. Continue mixing and adding water until mixture resembles fudge. Taste and add more sugar, vanilla, or peanut butter if necessary. Press into a fry pan and chill.

Variations: Add chopped nuts or chocolate chips.

Frostings

QUICK TOPPING

Sprinkle 2 Tbs. brown sugar, ¼ tsp. cinnamon, and 2 Tbs. margarine on top of cake when done, put lid back on, and bake a few more minutes until margarine melts.

CHOCOLATE FROSTING

½ cup cocoa mix
¼ to ½ cup brown sugar
4 Tbs. margarine, melted
2 Tbs. water (or coffee for mocha)

Combine all ingredients and cook on low heat, stirring vigorously. Add nuts, fruit, or coconut for variety. Pour over cake.

BUTTERSCOTCH FROSTING

½ cup brown sugar
4 Tbs. margarine, melted
4 Tbs. powdered milk
2 Tbs. water

Mix as above for chocolate frosting. If it seems granular, add another 1 Tbs. water and stir until it becomes more creamy.

ORANGE FROSTING

4 Tbs. margarine
⅓ cup brown sugar
½ cup orange fruit drink crystals
3 Tbs. water
3 Tbs. powdered milk

Heat margarine, sugar, and fruit crystals over moderate heat, stirring. Mix water and milk and add to mixture after margarine melts. Simmer about 5 minutes until thickened. Add more water if too thick. Take off heat, let set 1 minute, and spread on cake.

Variation: Add ¼ cup coconut.

Cookies

BASIC COOKIES (makes 9 3-inch cookies)

½ cup brown sugar
¼ cup margarine
¼ cup powdered milk
3 Tbs. water
¾ cup baking mix (see page 63)
½ cup white flour
⅛ tsp. salt

Cream sugar and margarine together. Mix milk powder and water and add to sugar mixture. Combine flour, salt, and baking mix and add to other ingredients, working it into a stiff dough. Divide into nine pieces. Flatten and bake for about 10 minutes, using a twiggy fire.

Variations:

- Cinnamon: Sprinkle mixture of 1½ Tbs. brown sugar and ½ tsp. cinnamon over cookies before baking.
- Fruit and nut: Mix ½ cup (total) of your choice of fruit, nuts, and seeds into dough.
- Chocolate/carob chips: Add 1 tsp. vanilla, ⅓ cup chocolate or carob chips, and ¼ cup chopped walnuts.
- Peanut butter: Omit salt, add 4 Tbs. peanut butter, 2 Tbs. more flour, and ¼ cup chopped peanuts.
- Chocolate: Add ½ cup cocoa and 4 Tbs. water instead of powdered milk mixture.

NITTY GRITTY CORNMEAL COOKIES
(makes 12 to 15 2½-inch cookies)

½ cup margarine
6 Tbs. brown sugar
⅔ cup + 1 Tbs. flour
⅓ cup cornmeal
½ to 1 tsp. vanilla
pinch of salt
extra cornmeal for rolling

Combine margarine and brown sugar. Add other ingredients to form a stiff dough. Roll 1 Tbs. dough into a ball. Roll it in the extra cornmeal. Flatten to ¼-inch thickness. Bake, using a twiggy fire, for 8 to 10 minutes or until done. Cool for a moment before removing from pan.

GRANOLA CHEWIES
(makes about 12 3-inch cookies or 2 pan-size ones)

1 cup granola
¾ cup flour
½ cup brown sugar (or 6 Tbs. sugar + 2 Tbs. honey)
½ cup margarine
2 Tbs. powdered egg mixed with 2 Tbs. water
½ tsp. salt
½ tsp. baking powder
½ tsp. vanilla

Mix ingredients together and drop by spoonfuls into a frying pan. Cover and bake, using a twiggy fire, for 8 to 10 minutes. Cookies will set as they cool.

OATMEAL CRACKERS
(makes 24 to 30 1½-inch squares)

3 Tbs. powdered milk
4 Tbs. water
¼ cup margarine
¼ cup brown sugar
½ tsp. vanilla
1 cup oatmeal
1 cup + 2 Tbs. flour
¾ tsp. baking powder
pinch salt

Mix milk powder and water; add to creamed margarine and brown sugar. Add vanilla and stir in oatmeal. Mix flour, baking powder, and salt together and add to mixture. Dough should hold together but not be sticky. Add a bit more milk or flour if needed to achieve proper consistency. Roll half the dough as thin as possible and cut into 1- to 2-inch squares. Put crackers into a heated, slightly oiled fry pan. Cook, covered, for 6 to 8 minutes using a twiggy fire, or fry on both sides. Repeat with remaining dough. These are good plain or with cheese, wild berry jam, or peanut butter spread.

NUTTY SANDIES (makes 20 to 24 cookies)

A good way to use up extra margarine, flour, and nuts.

3 cups flour (white or mostly white works best)
1½ cups margarine
¾ cup brown sugar
⅔ cup finely chopped nuts (almonds are best)
1 tsp. vanilla

Mix ingredients into a dough with your hands. Break off spoon-size pieces. Roll into balls and flatten. Fry in a heated, dry pan for about 4 minutes on each side or bake in a covered pan, using a twiggy fire, for about 8 to 10 minutes. Baked version is more cookie-like. Fried version should sit a few minutes after cooking to set.

NO-BAKE ESKIMO COOKIES
(makes about 16 cookies)

1 cup oatmeal
6 Tbs. margarine
6 Tbs. brown sugar
3 Tbs. cocoa mix
½ tsp. vanilla
½ Tbs. water

Mix all ingredients together. Form into walnut-sized balls. Eat immediately or let sit in a cool place.
   Variation: Roll in a combination of 1 Tbs. powdered milk and 1 Tbs. brown sugar, or in coconut.

NO-BAKE POWERHOUSE COOKIES
(makes 20 to 24 cookies)

Our taste testers loved these!

1 cup brown sugar
¼ cup margarine
3 Tbs. powdered milk
4 Tbs. water
1 cup oatmeal
1 cup peanut butter
½ cup nuts
¼ cup chocolate or carob chips
½ tsp. vanilla

Mix sugar, margarine, powdered milk, and water in a pan. Bring to a boil. Reduce heat and boil 3 minutes, stirring constantly to prevent scorching. Remove from heat and stir in remaining ingredients. Drop by spoonfuls onto a flat surface such as a pan lid. Let sit for about 10 minutes to set. In hot weather, they might not set as well.

CHEWY FUDGE NO-BAKE COOKIES
(makes about 20 to 24 cookies)

1 cup brown sugar
¼ cup cocoa mix
5 Tbs. margarine
3 Tbs. powdered milk
3 Tbs. water
1½ cups oatmeal
¼ cup nuts
½ tsp. vanilla

Mix sugar, margarine, cocoa, and milk (made from the milk powder and water) together in a pan. Follow same procedure as for no-bake powerhouse cookies (above).

Pies

EASY CRUST (for a 12-inch pan)

4 Tbs. margarine
⅔ to 1 cup flour
2 Tbs. brown sugar
¼ tsp. salt

Melt margarine and mix in other ingredients until crust is consistency of a graham cracker crust—not greasy, but a bit dry. Pat into bottom of a frying pan and bake 5 to 10 minutes or until golden brown. Cool and add a cooked fruit filling or an instant pudding.

Variation: Pies can also be made with a rolled crust. See instructions under the quiche moraine recipe in the dinners section.

FRUIT PIE FILLING

1½ cups dried fruit
2 cups water
pinch salt
½ to ⅔ cup sugar (to taste, depending on fruit used)
1 tsp. cinnamon or nutmeg
2 Tbs. margarine
2 to 3 Tbs. flour
½ cup chopped nuts

Simmer fruit in water until hydrated. Drain off all juice except about ½ cup. Save drained juice. Add margarine, salt, sugar, and spice to fruit. Stir well. Mix flour with drained-off juice (about ⅓ cup) and stir into fruit. Add nuts. Simmer, stirring often, until thickened. Pour into an already baked crust and allow to set. Garnish with granola or Grapenuts.

Variation: This can be made with fresh fruit or berries. Increase the amount of fruit and decrease the water. Adjust with a thickener.

Specialty Snacks

RICE PUDDING (serves 3 to 4)

2 cups cooked brown or white rice
²⁄₃ cup powdered milk
½ cup raisins
6 Tbs. brown sugar or honey
2 fresh eggs, beaten, or 1½ Tbs. powdered egg*
½ tsp. cinnamon
1⅓ cups water
½ to 1½ tsp. vanilla (depending on strength)

Combine all ingredients except vanilla. Cook over low heat, stirring constantly, until thickened—about 10 to 15 minutes. *Do not boil.* Stir in vanilla.

Variation: Stir in ¼ to ½ cup peanut butter as it cooks.

*Note: If using powdered egg, mix 1½ Tbs. flour with egg and add some water. Pour mixture into rice and cook.

IAN'S ICE CREAM

Fill a mug with fresh snow (1½ cups). Stir in 2 Tbs. powdered milk, 1 Tbs. brown sugar, and ½ to 1 tsp. vanilla. Stir until creamy.

Variations:

- Chocolate: Omit brown sugar and add 2 Tbs. cocoa mix.
- Fruit: Omit sugar and vanilla and add 1 Tbs. lemon or orange fruit crystals—it's tangier without the powdered milk.
- Apple: Omit sugar and vanilla and add 1 Tbs. apple cider mix and a dash of cinnamon.

* Cheesecake: Omit sugar and vanilla and add 1 to 2 Tbs. cheesecake mix.

PEANUT BRITTLE/PEANUT POPCORN

2 Tbs. margarine
½ to 1 cup brown sugar
1 cup peanuts or popped popcorn
pinch salt

Melt margarine. Dissolve sugar in it, stirring constantly while cooking. When a small spoonful of the hot sugar mixture forms a ball upon being dropped into cold water, it is done. Add peanuts or popped popcorn and salt; stir; cool immediately by placing pan in snow or cold water.

CARAMELS/CHOCOLATE CARAMELS

3 Tbs. water
½ cup powdered milk
2 Tbs. cocoa mix (for chocolate version)
1 cup brown sugar
3 Tbs. margarine
1 cup nuts, seeds, or popped popcorn

Mix water into powdered milk and cocoa. Follow directions for peanut brittle, adding milk mixture after sugar has dissolved and continuing to cook. If mixture is granular, add 1 to 2 Tbs. water and it will smooth out. You can drop spoonfuls of the mixture onto a pot lid or onto hard snow and let them set.

POPCORN

1 Tbs. oil (margarine will work if you are careful)
½ cup popcorn

Heat oil in frying pan with a lid. Add a few kernels of popcorn. When they pop, add popcorn and cover. Place pan over hot coals or stove and shake until popping subsides. Salt popcorn or sprinkle with soy sauce and nutritional yeast. Or add cayenne and cumin to some melted margarine and pour over popcorn.

ROASTED NUTS AND SEEDS

Heat a fry pan. Add raw nuts or seeds and dry-roast, stirring to prevent burning. Sprinkle with salt or soy sauce.

Recipe Index